"Once again, in his second book, *A Table For Two*, Dean Johnson touches the world with love!"

—ADONI MAROPIS, actor, lead villain, Fayed, in hit series "24"

"Congratulations Dean! *A Table For Two* is a masterpiece! I'm impressed by the intelligence behind it. It's quite an achievement. How you share the stories of your life, especially those relating to table tennis is something to be proud of."

—TIM BOGGAN, USA Table Tennis Historian

"*A Table for Two* is an amazing, inspirational chronicle of the life of author Dean Johnson. Dean shares his experiences, recurring relationships and connections in his personal and professional life with the sport of table tennis. His accounts are to the point of being more than mere coincidence or serendipitous in nature but closer to the Chinese concept known as 'Yuan fen' (缘分). *A Table For Two* highlights the lifelong health benefits associated with the sport as it applied to his life over and over again. This is a 'must read'—not the usual book on a sport or healthy living. Wrap your eyes, heart and mind around this 5-star gem."

—MICHAEL L. BABUIN, PG, PhD; Past Chairman of the Board
USA Table Tennis

"Dean Johnson's *A Table for Two* is an autobiographical pongfest that starts with this Hall of Famer's beginnings, then delves into his personal interactions and photos with many of the greats of Table Tennis—Marty Reisman, Dick Miles, Sol Schiff, Leah Neuberger, Patty Martinez and Stellan Bengtsson. It also provides golden nuggets on the book's subtitle: 'How the sport of table tennis provides fitness and can add years to your life.'"

—LARRY HODGES, Table Tennis Hall of Famer, Coach and author

"Dean Johnson's contributions to the sport of table tennis are legendary. His six-volume *American Table Tennis During The Classic Age* is a definitive history of the sport between 1931 & 1966. His current book *A Table For Two* is a brilliant autobiography of his life in, and love of the sport of table tennis. Anyone who has ever played the game can benefit from reading *A Table for Two*, not so much about how the game of table tennis is played but about how the game of life is played. His belief in 'just show up' is a shining example."

—DICK EVANS, former president of the USATT Hall of Fame Board of Directors

A Table for Two
by Dean Johnson

ISBN 978-1-63393-798-7

Published by

◤ köehlerbooks™

210 60th Street
Virginia Beach, VA 23451
800–435–4811
www.koehlerbooks.com

A TABLE
FOR TWO

How the sport of table tennis provides
physical fitness and can add years to your life.

DEAN JOHNSON

VIRGINIA BEACH
CAPE CHARLES

CHAPTER TITLE	PAGE

FOREWORD I

Rev. Dr. David B. Antonson

Dean Johnson's book, *A Table For Two*, touches on the many dimensions of Dean's life—his contributions in graphic arts, his life in the military, his love of table tennis and tennis, his love of his family and his wife, Helga. But most of all, Dean has a keen eye to see how all the pieces fit together.

Dean shows us how a person can listen to their life, the way a doctor listens through his stethoscope to what's going on in our body. Dean is aware that a providential hand has guided his life, there is an order, nothing is wasted, everything means something, and all that builds over time. Throughout his book there is a sense of gratitude for the people he has known and worked with, and how those friendships have enriched him.

Dean and I share a Norwegian background; a number of years ago, my wife and I visited that wonderful Norwegian Folk Museum on the outskirts of Oslo, Norway located at Bygdoy. It is a collection of 160 buildings from all over the country. I noticed in one house, hand-carved above the door with a pocket knife, were the words, "The Lord will keep you from all harm—he will watch over your life; the Lord will watch over your coming and going, both now and forevermore." (Psalm 121:7,8)

This great Psalm has often been called the traveler's psalm, because it is a reminder that the Almighty guides our footsteps, is out ahead of us leading the way. The owner of the house wanted that daily reminder, that their life was part of a great plan, as he or she headed out on their daily chores.

I especially like the way Dean brings so many of his thoughts and experiences together at the end, "Life's Lessons Learned." He lists nine of them. His book is not "preachy" as some would think of it, but with a keen eye, he shows how God has been at work in his life. In many ways, it is a testimony to the goodness of God in his life.

About six years ago I had the privilege of working with a key business person in Pittsburgh. He had many achievements to celebrate. He has been instrumental in his church chairing a large capital campaign that completely changed the life and mission of that church. He said one day, "I keep on my desk, a two-word reminder of what my life is about: 'Everything Counts.'"

I want to commend Dean for collecting in one place the stories and photos that have guided his life. A lot of us think about doing this someday, but Dean has done it and done it well.

Thank you, Dean; I hope that this book has wide circulation. We will all benefit.

David B. Antonson

David B. Antonson is an ordained Presbyterian minister living in Lincoln, California. He and his wife, Judy, grew up in Duluth, Minnesota. He is a graduate of the University of Minnesota (Duluth campus), Columbia Theological Seminary in Decatur, Georgia and McCormick Theological Seminary in Chicago. He has served a total of nine Presbyterian congregations of all sizes in Alabama, Michigan, and Pennsylvania.

FOREWORD II

Scott Sautter Ph. D.

On a rainswept, stormy day, I had the honor and pleasure to spend what turned out to be a most memorable trip riding with Dean Johnson to a table tennis event on the Eastern Shore of Virginia. That is because Dean told many stories that were, in essence, a sneak preview to this book, *A Table For Two*.

Within the pages of this book, Dean's life unfolds and intersects with so many others, including the who's who of table tennis.

Dean likes to quote Woody Allen that "80% of life is showing up," as if just by showing up Dean has made things happen in many successful ways.

One such event occurred when he was on *The Hampton Roads Show*, a morning variety show that was featuring the annual Ping Pong for Charity fundraiser. The host of the show, Chris Reckling, was interviewing Ken Lees, President of the Table Tennis Charity Foundation.

He then turned to Dean and put a microphone in front of him and asked, "Dr. Sautter, how is ping-pong related to brain health?" Without skipping a beat, Dean launched into ping-pong and brain fitness so seamlessly that the host never knew that Dean was not Dr. Sautter!

Another memorable event occurred at the Eastern Virginia Medical School following a table tennis exhibition Dean was playing, when he was asked if he was interested in attending a medical student program about aging. Dean found himself not just attending the program. He *was* The Program, sitting with the faculty on the panel while students were asking him questions about aging.

Throughout this book, Dean shares his remarkable life and the wonderful connections he has made, from when he was a young man through his time in the military to meeting his wife, through his professional career and the balance he had achieved by playing and competing in table tennis.

Dean's book is a fascinating history of multiple characters, family members and friends that have shaped his life. Whether the events initially appear to be positive or negative, Dean has an expectation of coherence, that things will reasonably work out regardless of the circumstance, a very salutogenic perspective!

Although it seems that so many positive and successful things happened to him just because he showed up, he reminds the reader that this was only by the hand of God that placed him in these circumstances. Dean's "just showing up" strategy has really been his trust in God that his life circumstances will work out in a reasonably positive manner because he has learned to listen and allow these circumstances to take place.

I think Dean would agree with Psalms 46:10, "Be still, and know that I am God," as a defining philosophy of how he has lived his life. Life is not random events coincidentally occurring but divinely inspired.

                                                              Scott Sautter Ph. D.

Dr. Sautter received his Ph.D. from Vanderbilt University and post-doctoral fellowship in neuropsychology at the University of Virginia School of Medicine. He is the past chair of the Medical and Scientific Committee of the Southeastern Virginia Chapter of the Alzheimer's Association, past president of the American Board of Professional Neuropsychology, and is on the community faculty with the Eastern Virginia Medical School as an assistant professor. He currently serves as the chair of the Table Tennis Charity Foundation.

INTRODUCTION

Throughout history, many scientists have believed that there is far more to life than the blind interactions of matter and energy. There is something about the universe that cannot be explained just by the impersonal forces of nature and atoms colliding with atoms. We must reach beyond the universe to account for it.

Albert Einstein once wrote, "The religious inclination dwells in humans that all nature, including the humans in it, is in no way an accidental game, but a work of lawfulness that there is a fundamental *purpose* to all existence."

Einstein's belief in an *Intelligent Designer* derived not from a preconceived religious bias, but from the phenomenal insights into the universe that he possessed as the most brilliant scientist who ever lived.

In a 1930 essay entitled *What I Believe*, Einstein wrote, "To sense that behind anything that can be experienced there is something that our minds cannot grasp, whose beauty and sublimity reaches us only indirectly; this is religiousness. In this sense, and in this sense only, I am a devoutly religious man."

If there is a "fundamental purpose to all existence," as Einstein believes, what does that mean for us? If there is a "fundamental purpose to all of existence," why not purpose to each of our lives?

I believe that in my eighty-seven years, as I try to demonstrate and offer examples in this book, I have experienced the presence of a *Divine Intelligence* that has guided my life, *Divinely Inspired* events that have had a profound influence on my path—experiences, I believe, that cannot be explained away as mere "good luck," "coincidence," or "serendipity."

The heart of the message you'll find in *A Table For Two* is the life-long benefits that can be derived from participating in the sport of table tennis. Table tennis is a sport about which I've been passionate for more than 60 years, and for which I credit my relatively good health in approaching my 90th year.

Table tennis is a relatively inexpensive sport, it's safe and can begin to be taught as early as four or five years of age. I personally know of men and women now playing well into their 90s.

Built around the message of the benefits of table tennis is a series of autobiographical stories—stories of events and of lives that I believe to be divinely inspired—events that began long before I was born—and on the lives of close friends and acquaintances whom I believe to border on genius.

I believe that you'll find this book reads like a Russian novel and at the same time has a message that could add years to your life.

———————————

Whatever led to an early-1920s decision by a couple named Mary and Michael Donohue, living in Garfield, New Jersey, to build a house three miles to the south on Bloomfield Avenue in Clifton marked the beginning of an incredible story about how a series of Divinely Inspired events, starting with this relocation, determined the path of my life.

Michael and Mary Donohue, circa 1920s.

Proximity of Johnson (l) and Donohue (r) homes. (Some 90 years after they were built.) Google image,

THE DONOHUES MOVE

The location of the Donohues' new home happened to be just a block and a half from a couple of Swedish and Norwegian origin who owned a home on six acres of farmland named Anna Marie Pedersdatter Varlof Johnson and Carl Fritioff (Fred) Johnson. This decision by Mary and Michael Donohue to build at this location led to the creation of several new generations of Johnsons—an event I believe was Divinely Inspired.

The Donohues had two children, a girl and a boy—Helen and John. Mary had two other children—Lillian and Mae—by a previous marriage to William Flynn. Helen, my mother, was ten years old at the time the Donohues moved from Garfield to Clifton, New Jersey.

Michael, along with two of his brothers, James and Patrick, made fortunes during prohibition. In addition to owning speakeasies, Michael was also a professional boxer and boxing promoter. Another of Michael's brothers, Thomas, was City Clerk of nearby Passaic.

(lower left) Original Johnson home built in 1904 and in which four of the six Johnson boys were born. (lower right) New home under construction in 1909. How the years passed by.

On April 16, 1898, my paternal grandparents Fred Johnson and Anna Marie Warlo, recent immigrants from Scandinavia, were married in New York City. In 1899, Anna and Fred moved to Passaic, New Jersey, and in 1903, they bought a six-acre plot on Bloomfield Avenue in Clifton on which they built a small house (lower left). In 1909, they built another, larger home on the lot (lower right). The old house was then converted to a garage.

The *Divinely Inspired* proximity of these homes in the 1930s—and the interaction of the two families living there—the Donohues and the Johnsons—had an enormous impact on the destiny of these families for generations to come. The proximity of this home to the Donohue home built in 1921 was what led to the connection and eventual marriage of my parents, Dean Alfred Johnson and Helen Donohue, on April 5, 1931.

Four of Anna and Fred's six sons were born in the first house—LeRoy, Edward, Floyd, and Howard. Dean and Victor were born in the new larger home. Photo on the previous page circa 1916. How the years passed by.

In the early 1920s, a well-to-do couple named Mary and Michael Donohue moved from Hepworth Place in Garfield to a home they had built on Broadway in Passaic a block and a half from the Johnsons. This relocation was the first of what I believe to be the many Divinely Inspired events that have lit my path for more than eighty-seven years.

THE SELF-RELIANCE OF ANNA & FRED JOHNSON

My paternal grandparents, Fred Johnson and Anna Marie Warlo Johnson, who were neighbors of the Donohues, were models of self-reliance and role models for the entire Johnson family.

Anna Marie was raised in a small farming commune, Eiker, Buskerud, thirty miles west of Oslo, Norway. Sometime in the 1870s, the family moved to Oslo and, when Anna finished school, she found a job and worked hard to save for passage to America.

Fred and Anna circa 1895–1948. How the years passed by.

Fred's childhood home in Segerstad Parish, Sweden; soon after Fred left the Varmland homestead where he was born, his brother Algot had the above photo taken circa 1900. Shown in the photo are Algot and the boys' mother, Britta-Lisa. The home was sold by Algot in 1910 when he moved to Hammaron, but the basic structure of the house, though oft remodeled, remains at the same location, and occupied.

The home as it was when I visited on August 21, 1996. Here I'm sitting with the home's occupant at the time, Brita Eklof.

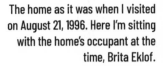

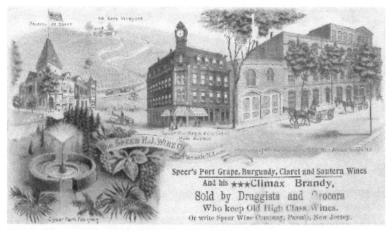

In 1898 Fred was employed by winemaker Alfred Speer in Passaic, New Jersey for whom he drove a team of horses as those shown in the postcard above.

In May 1892, at age twenty-four, Anna emigrated from Norway to the U.S. From 1892–1897, she lived and worked in New York City. Judging by the collection of her early photos on page sixteen, she may have spent some of that time employed as a fashion model.

In 1896, Anna returned to Norway to visit relatives where she met Carl Frithiof Jansson (later known as Fred) who had earlier emigrated from Karlstad, Sweden to Oslo. In 1896, Anna returned to the U.S., and a year later, Fred joined her.

From 1897–1899, Fred and Anna lived in Poughkeepsie, New York. Fred worked as a gardener and Anna as a housekeeper for a family named Green who owned the *Hotel Metropole* located at 147 West 43rd Street just off Times Square in New York City. The Greens also owned a summer home in Katohah, New York.

On April 16, 1898, Fred and Anna married. At the time, Fred was employed by winemaker Alfred Speer, for whom he drove a team of horses; he then joined *Latham Foundry* in Passaic. Fred's last job was with *Robbins Conveyor* in Passaic, where he worked as a cast-iron molder from 1904 until 1947, at which time he retired at the age of seventy-nine.

Anna's birthplace in Norway; Hokksund is a town in the municipality of Øvre Eiker in the county of Buskerud in Norway. Hokksund is the administrative center and the largest town in the municipality. The map shows the location of the three Varlo farms, on one of which Anna Varlo (Warloe) was born.

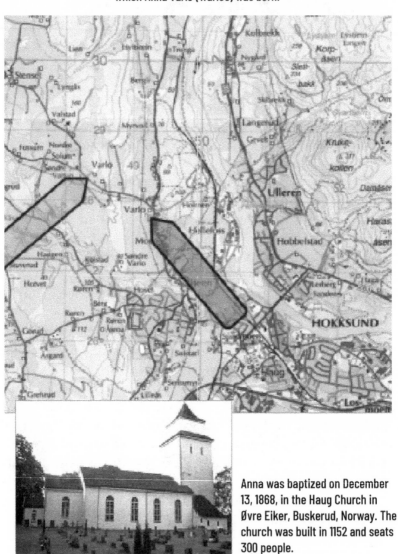

Anna was baptized on December 13, 1868, in the Haug Church in Øvre Eiker, Buskerud, Norway. The church was built in 1152 and seats 300 people.

Anna's childhood home in Oslo, Norway: The Identities of the people on the balconies in this home (which Anna identified as her home in Oslo) can only be conjecture. But my guess starts with the fact that Anna Marie Warloe was twenty-four when she immigrated to America in 1892. Assuming she's in this photo, she would have to be a young girl.
Perhaps she is the girl on the top balcony to the left, who appears to be about ten.
If that is the case, this photo would be circa the late 1870s. That would make the couple in the middle about the right age to be Anna's parents (Peder late thirties and Andrine Skinstad early thirties). Peder could be holding Nicoline, about whom we know nothing. The woman on the left holding the cat could be either Peder's mother or Andrine's mother both of whom would be in their mid-late seventies.

Judging by this collection of Anna's early photos she may have spent some of her late teens and early twenties working as a fashion model. The photo in the upper left was taken in 1887, when she was nineteen and still living in Oslo. The others were taken between 1892 and 1897, when she was living and working in New York. Her maiden name was Anna Varlo, after the farm on which she was born. Captions on the photos are in her handwriting. How pleased she would be to know that after 130 years her photos have been preserved and shared.

The Johnson boys in 1918—Floyd, Howard, LeRoy, Victor, Edward and Dean—prior to Edward leaving to serve in the Navy during World War I.

Family researchers report that Anna was told by a relative who owned a boarding house in Oslo that she had a Swedish guest staying at her place—someone she might like to meet. His name was Carl Frithiof Jansson. Anna and Carl (who later became known as Fred) exchanged photos—apparently to each other's satisfaction, for in 1897 Anna returned to Oslo, where she met Fred. Anna returned to New York and Fred followed a year later. They were married on April 16, 1898. In 1899, Anna and Fred moved to Passaic, New Jersey. In 1903, they bought a six-acre plot on Bloomfield Avenue in Clifton for $3,000.

While working full-time in a foundry, Fred built a small house on the lot. He and Anna wasted no time turning it into a farm where they raised chickens, pigs, and cows; grew their own vegetables, fruits, and fruit trees; and had a vineyard of red and white grapes from which Fred made his own wine. As I was growing up in the 1930s, the farmland was a vacant lot, but the vineyard was still there and Anna's garden was lush with flowers.

A sixty-seven-year leap ahead. The Johnson boys on July 31, 1985—Floyd, Howard, LeRoy (sitting), Victor, Edward and Dean Alfred. How the years passed by.

The resourcefulness, the determination, the independence and self-reliance that Anna showed from the time she left her home as a teenager in Oslo until she and Fred were settled in their own home in Clifton is a story of strength and fortitude.

Fred and Anna worked hard all their lives. Anna made every penny count—she was a wonderful mother, cook, housekeeper, gardener, and, to me, a spiritual beacon.

Fred worked in the foundry for forty-three years, hardly missing a day. At home he kept the houses he built in good repair and even found time to repair his six boys' shoes in his basement.

The home he designed and had built in the 1920s is, at this writing, being considered as a "Historic Landmark" in Clifton.

Fred and Anna did not have a whole lot to say to each other. My mother told me that for a period of seven years they didn't speak at all.

Fred had a few friends like Martin Munch and John Lundstead; Anna had her Bible. During that time, if they communicated at all, it was through third parties. Occasionally, I was the third party. One day Fred said to me, when the three of us were alone in the kitchen, "Tell the old woman I'm going to see Martin Munch."

On December 31, 1946, Fred spoke to Anna. He said, "Don't make my lunch." From those few words, she knew that after forty-three years at *Robbins Conveyor*, he had retired.

Fred and Anna, by all appearances, did not seem to be close. But when Anna died, Fred cried.

When Fred turned 94, he was interviewed by a local newspaper. The reporter asked him, "how does it feel, Mr. Johnson, to live to be your age?"

In his Swedish accent, he replied, "I think about how fast by it went."

Fred and Anna with grandson Dean home on leave March, 1954.

Fred on the day of Anna's funeral. Anna died on my twenty-seventh birthday, January 21, 1959.

VICTOR JOHNSON & JOHN DONOHUE, ROLE MODELS

During my formative years I didn't get to spend much quality time my father but I was blessed with two surrogate fathers—Uncle Vic on the Johnson side and John on the Donohue side, both of whom spent generous amounts of quality time with me. Vic took me with him everywhere—on his motorcycle, his airplane and his truck.

Uncle John (pages 25–26), with his talent, athletic skills, and likable disposition, was also a positive role model for me.

(Top right) On Vic's motorcycle in the spring of 1935, Vic with model airplanes he built as a teenager circa 1928. (bottom left) Vic introduced me to photography in 1933. (bottom right) Vic at the controls of North American B-25 Mitchell Bomber. During WW II, while in the Air Transport Command, Vic ferried aircraft, freight and military personnel.

THE HERALD NEWS

70th Year in the Public's Service　　　24 Pages　　　PASSAIC, N.J., MONDAY, OCTOBER 20, 1941

Plane Falls on Bergen Highway, Pilot Crushed

LUCKY - Victor Johnson, of Allwood, escaped with his life this morning in a plane crash in the East Rutherford meadows. The pilot was killed. Johnson suffered a broken arm and shock.

CASUALTY. Victor Johnson, also a flying instructor, is helped from crashed plane. Ship struck wires, hit two cars, before cracking up.

When Vic arrived at the emergency room of Hackensack Hospital, the doctor on duty prepared him for amputation of his right arm. When Vic's friend Ed Gorski arrived at the hospital and learned what the doctors were about to do, he summoned a student-pilot of his, who happened to be an orthopedic surgeon, to come to the hospital immediately. The skilled surgeon took charge of the situation and was able to save Vic's arm. Vic was forever grateful to Ed Gorski and his surgeon friend for their quick, decisive action. (Family trivia: Ed Gorski was married to the sister of Jimmy Donohue's wife Anna Chizacky.)

Despite suffering horrific injuries in this October 19, 1941 crash, Vic volunteered his services and flying skills to the war effort less than a year after the accident.

EARLY FRIENDS & AN INSPIRED RELOCATION

When I was born in January 1932, the country was in the depths of the Depression. The company for whom my father was working in 1931, *Fokker Aircraft* in Teterboro, New Jersey, was absorbed by the *Aircraft Division of General Motors* in Baltimore, so my parents (my mother now pregnant with me) relocated to a row house there.

While we were there my grandmother Anna traveled often to Baltimore by train to help my twenty-year old mother care for me, Anna's thirty-two-year-old son LeRoy, and a boarder my parents took in to help pay the rent.

But Helen found life too difficult in Baltimore, so in November 1933, she and I moved back to Clifton to live with her parents— the Donohues—on Bloomfield Avenue in Passaic. Following that relocation, we lived in relative luxury and comfort. My father moved from job to job—from vacuum cleaner salesman to magazine truck driver to "counter" man at one of the Donohues' road-stands in Union, New Jersey. These jobs, according to my mother, were among the more than twenty my father held during his career.

We lived with the Donohues' until November 1, 1934, at which time Mom and Dad reconciled and they moved to the *Lincoln Apartments* on Broadway in Passaic.

After living here until April 1, 1935 and with another child on the way, we clearly needed more space.

My grandmother Donohue was a longtime friend of a woman named Eliza Murray Coates. Eliza and her family lived just a block and a half down Scoles Avenue from the Donohues.

When my grandmother Donohue told Eliza that her daughter was looking for a place to rent, Eliza told her that a house next to her on Scoles Avenue was available. My mother contacted the owner, Jennie Brown, about availability and price; Brown was asking $25/month. My mother and father agreed to her terms, and on April 1, 1935, we all moved to a modest rental at 87 Scoles Avenue in

Clifton—next door to the Coates family!

This relocation, clearly Divinely Inspired, was to have a profound impact on the Johnson family for generations to come.

Twenty-year-old Helen and one-year-old Dean Robert (aka Bobby) not happy in Baltimore.

Helen at Scoles Avenue home in 1937: Helen and husband Dean lived here with Dean Robert and newborn Raymond from 1935 until September 1941. This was how the house looked in 2003. Not much different from the day Dean and Helen rented it for $25 per month in 1935. The walkway on which Helen is standing is between our house and the Coates' family house. Behind the house was farmland where cows grazed. One day on this very walkway, Helen met a cow coming from the opposite direction. She told me she nearly fainted at the sight.

HELEN & JOHN DONOHUE

Helen Donohue, my mother, was born on May 4, 1911 in Passaic, New Jersey. Her brother, John, was born on April 4, 1913 in Garfield. All their lives they were very close; they supported each other. I was blessed to have Helen for a mother and John for an uncle.

I think my mother was a saint for the way she endured the many hardships she faced in her marriage. She was raised in a well-to-do family but from the time she was married at twenty until she died at seventy-nine, her life was a constant struggle. Yet she handled it with patience and Grace and prayer.

Every night she would pray with me, "Now I lay me down to sleep, I pray the Lord my soul to keep, if I should die before I wake, I pray the Lord my soul to take." That was followed by a blessing for every family member: *God bless Gammy and Pop, God bless Gram and Mike, God bless Uncle John*—and so it would go until every family member was blessed. Then she would say to me, "Now let's be quiet and listen to God." I didn't know what she meant then; but I know now. It's called meditation.

The last words Ma said to me before she died were "Jesus suffered, why shouldn't I?" John and Helen died within five weeks of each other in June and July 1990.

As a youth, John Donohue had "Hollywood" good looks. As an athlete, he was so talented he might have been a major-league baseball player.

As a singer, he had such a good voice, he might have been a crooner; better than Crosby, as good as Sinatra.

"For of all sad words of tongue or pen, the saddest are these: It might have been!" as John Greenleaf Whittier wrote.

"I had it too good and was just too lazy, Bob. I didn't use the gifts I was given," he once confessed to me.

GRAND-UNCLE JIMMY DONOHUE & HIS FRIEND BABE RUTH

As a youth, I was impressed and inspired by my Grand-Uncle Jimmy Donohue. Jimmy started in the bar-and-restaurant business when he inherited a hotel from his father which was originally called the *John J. Donohue Hotel*. Later, the name was changed to the *Black Sea Hotel* in Garfield, New Jersey. As my Uncle John told me:

"In the mid-1920s, a trainer for the New York Yankees baseball team stumbled on the *Black Sea*. He told a member of the team, Babe Ruth, that he had found a 'hideaway' for him. A short drive from Yankee Stadium, the 'Babe' found the *Black Sea* to his liking—and he began to spend time there, partaking of adult refreshments and Jimmy's famous hot dogs, away from the crowds who incessantly hounded him for autographs.

"For a while the Babe was able to enjoy the solitude of the *Black Sea*, but inevitably word got around that Ruth was a patron. Ruth's big car, which bore New York license plates, was often seen outside. Fans started to flock, and Ruth took off.

"However, Jimmy and the Bambino had grown to be close friends, and Jimmy wasn't going to lose Ruth if he could help it. There was a garage across the street from the hotel, which Jimmy bought and had it fixed up as private quarters for Ruth.

"When the Babe was able to drive right into the garage without being seen, he came back. Jimmy assigned a waiter to Ruth who would carry food and drinks over to the garage.

"The arrangement suited the Babe just fine, and he and Jimmy remained close friends and visited each other until just a few days before the Babe's death in 1948."

In September 2001, I visited the location in Garfield that in the 1920s had been the *Black Sea Hotel* and was now the *Pescador* restaurant. I asked for the owner, introduced myself and asked her if I could see the room in the hotel reserved for Babe Ruth—before

Jimmy had the garage next door built for him. The room was no more than 10' X 10'—large enough for a bed and perhaps a chair and a table on which Babe could be served Jimmy's famous hot dogs, beer, and who knows what else.

Sometime in the 1930s, Jimmy relocated his establishment from Garfield to Route 23 in Mountain View, New Jersey. What started as a roadside stand there became one of the most famous restaurants and nightclubs in the State. At one time the restaurant was serving up 1,300 meals at dinner hour and patrons danced to some of the most famous big bands of the 1940s and '50s—Glen Miller, Tommy Dorsey and Harry James.

The restaurant also featured a fast-food counter for motorists, and who was one of those serving up the hot dogs to patrons in a white apron? None other than Jimmy himself!

Uncle Jim's "hands-on" approach and his personal relationship with customers had a profound impact on me. It was a model I tried to emulate during forty years of managing my own business.

I believe my relationship to Jimmy Donohue and the example he set for me was *Divinely Inspired.*

John J. Donohue Hotel, Garfield, New Jersey in the 1920s
and (inset) the Pescador hotel in 2001.

Grand Uncle Jimmy Donohue and Babe Ruth in 1938.

My personal recollection of Jimmy was of his humility and generosity. My mother was Jimmy's niece, and during occasional outings in the 1940s to Mountain View for a "roadside" dinner of Jimmy's famous hot dogs, the food would not only be "on the house" but Jimmy would slip a $20 bill to each member of the family—at a time when my father was making no more than $50/ week! Jimmy knew where his niece had come from and how she must have been struggling to make ends meet.

My Uncle John Donohue and Grand Uncle Jimmy Donohue when John worked for Jimmy in his nightclub in Mountain View, New Jersey in the mid-to-late 1930s.

Happy-go-lucky Jimmy tending bar at his nightclub in Mountain View. Jimmy was a friend and was loved by everyone!

Bobby and brother Ray engaging in some good natured sparring during construction of "Johnson's Ice Cream Bar" in 1946.

JOHNSON'S ICE CREAM BAR

As far back as I can remember (when I was known as "Bobby" to differentiate me from my father, Dean) I had an inclination toward self-reliance and entrepreneurship. For this, I credit the example set by my paternal grandparents Anna and Fred Johnson and my grand uncle Jimmy Donohue.

While still in elementary school, I worked in a variety of jobs, including assistant to the driver of a Dugan bread and cake delivery truck. This job, which started at 5:00 AM, was to drop off a loaf of bread and a coffee cake at each house at which the driver stopped. "If someone calls you," the driver instructed, "you didn't hear them." Although not totally ethical, I believe it was a very successful sales strategy for the driver—he chose to ask forgiveness rather than permission—a business strategy I learned from him and employed throughout my career.

I also shoveled coal in the winter for my parents' Jewish neighbors, the Simons, on Katherine Avenue. Their religion prohibited them from working on a Saturday. I was happy to receive two cents for the day.

I was also an assistant to a man named Al Nudak who had the newspaper route in our neighborhood and I operated a lemonade stand on Bloomfield Avenue in the summer and, while still in elementary school, I was a golf caddie at nearby *Upper Montclair Country Club.*

During high school, I did sign painting on trucks. I also developed a postcard/direct mail campaign for neighbor Jack Brady, who did architectural renderings of homes in the wealthy 3rd Ward Park section of Passaic. My inclination toward entrepreneurship also had to do, perhaps, with how poor our family was in the 1930s and '40s. In these years, my father's salary ranged from $25–$50/week. Money was scarce in our family—every penny counted.

My first real job, at fifteen, was waiting tables and helping make ice cream at *Johnson's Ice Cream Bar,* which my father and uncle Floyd opened in 1946. I worked there part-time or full-time (for $1.00/hour) from 1947 to 1950, when, following high school graduation, I was hired as an intern by Louis Kniep's ad agency. I started that job with nothing to offer other than passion and, perhaps, some talent in graphic arts.

Aerial view taken by Anna and Fred's son Victor, late 1930s.

In 1903, Anna and Fred bought a six-acre plot on Bloomfield Avenue in Clifton for $3,000. (The deed, by the way, is in Anna's name.)

This aerial view shows the main house (top center of the photo) which was built in 1909; the original house, some twenty yards behind it, was later converted to a garage. The family lived here when Edward, Floyd, and Howard were born.

The small building behind the original house is an outhouse for those living there. The low building with the dark roof in the foreground is a two-bay storage shed and the building to the upper far left was a florist shop operated by Anna and Fred's son Floyd in the 1930s. During the war, it was used for air raid warden meetings; after the war it was the starting structure for Johnson's Ice Cream Bar. The property's six acres meant more than adequate parking space for future customers.

In 1946, in a stroke of brilliance, Bobby's uncle Floyd came up with the idea for the *ice cream store.* The essential elements were all in place—an existing building on Johnson property (formerly a florist) and six acres of property. I eavesdropped on the conversation on the night Floyd presented his idea to my father and showed him the plans for the building. On that night, the most productive phase of my father's life began. If truth be told, Dean's mother Anna and father Fred were a major influence in my father being involved in the partnership—a condition, I believe, for their use of the property.

The timing could not have been better. Throughout the 1930s and '40s, America was obsessed with all things ice cream. In New York alone, twenty million gallons of vanilla, chocolate, and strawberry were consumed in drug stores and soda fountains. A store devoted to mostly just ice cream—from banana splits to egg creams to chocolate malts, all served up by "soda jerks" like me— became famous and fabulously successful.

Dean R in 1946 a year before he started working on his first real job at Johnson's Ice Cream Bar.

Dean A in his white cap and apron, in front of the ice cream store with nieces Beatrice and Barbara in 1947.

Coates family (standing): George, Margaret, Harry, Mary, and Jack. (sitting): Harry, Lillian, and Eliza. This 1930s photo was taken at their home next to ours on Scoles Avenue in Clifton, New Jersey.

THE DONOHUE/COATES/BRENNAN CONNECTION

Attractive, with a great sense of humor, style and grace, Lillian (sitting center) was a shining star in the Coates family.

At a tennis tournament in 1932, she met a man named Frank Brennan. Frank was with the Postal Service at the time; but he was also *New Jersey State Men's Tennis Champion* and he gave private tennis lessons and strung rackets to supplement his Postal Service income.

Lillian took occasional tennis lessons from Frank, their friendship turned into a relationship, and they were married on August 12, 1939.

During their courtship, of course, Frank spent many hours at the Coates' home next door to my parents on Scoles Avenue in Clifton. Lillian and Frank became close friends of Helen and Dean's and occasional babysitters for me.

Frank Brennan, Sr.

Frank's life was changed forever in 1959 when he decided to attend the *Eastern Grass Court Championships* at *Orange Lawn Tennis Club* in South Orange, New Jersey.

Frank's intention was to watch the current Wimbledon champion Maria Bueno play. On that day Bueno played a fifteen-year-old named Billie Jean Moffitt. Moffitt lost the match, but Frank liked her style and told her that he believed she would become a great player some day.

When Frank learned that Billie's parents did not travel with her, he invited her to stay with him and his family. A generous, genius move by Frank!

Frank with Billie Jean King at Ramapo College, New Jersey in 1981. Photo by Dean Johnson.

Billie Jean accepted, and she slowly became part of the Brennan family and Frank became her coach. Frank coached Billie Jean during her Battle of the Sexes match with Bobby Riggs, with a prize of $100,000. It was held in Houston, Texas on September 20, 1973. Billie won the match 6-4, 6-3, 6-3. The publicity Frank earned from this event catapulted his career. In 1965, he opened the highly successful *Frank Brennan Tennis Center* in Upper Saddle River and in 1969, he founded the *Frank Brennan Summer Tennis School* in Mercersburg, Pennsylvania.

Many of the Brennan children attended Brennan camps, as did our children Eric, Karen, and Kristina, all of whom played college tennis.

What are the chances that Frank Brennan would have enjoyed this level of success and celebrity if on that day in 1959, he had not attended the Eastern Grass Court Championships at Orange Lawn Tennis Club? It was life-altering, and, I believe a Divinely Inspired event.

FRANK BRENNAN, JR.

Frank was named NCAA and ITA Coach of the Decade for the 1980s. Photo by Dean.

Frank Brennan and Lillian had ten children—Frank Jr., Kevin, Jeffrey, Eileen, Christopher, Mary, twins Coleen and James, Nancy, and Terrance.

Among them, Frank Jr. followed most closely in his father's footsteps and had a most extraordinary tennis coaching career.

In addition to establishing the highly successful Frank Brennan Tennis Academy at Peddie School in Hightstown, New Jersey, he was head coach of the Stanford Women's Tennis Team from 1979–2000, coaching Stanford to ten NCAA titles.

On September 15, 2006, Frank was inducted into the Women's Collegiate Tennis Hall of Fame. Following is some of the text from the event program:

After attending Indiana University where he was a standout on the men's tennis team, Brennan began his coaching career at Stanford in the 1979–1980 academic year.

Twice recognized by the ITA as Coach of the Decade, Brennan developed some of the finest collegiate and future professional players in the country, including nine NCAA singles champions.

In twenty-one seasons coaching the Stanford women's tennis team, Frank compiled an eye-popping 510-50 overall record (.911) -most wins of any coach in program history. He is a four-time ITA/ Wilson Intercollegiate Coach of the Year and led the Cardinal to ten NCAA championships, including six in a row from 1986–91 and four perfect seasons (1982, 1984, 1989 and 1990), and was named the Pac-12 Women's Tennis Coach of the Century.

Dean and Helga with Frank Jr., his mother Lillian and wife Terry following Frank's induction into the Women's Collegiate Tennis Hall of Fame in 2006.

Frank is a member of both the Stanford Athletics Hall of Fame and the USTA/International Tennis Hall of Fame.

Frank Brennan established a hallmark in women's collegiate tennis that may never be surpassed.

Frank is also well known for a great sense of humor. I received a wonderful congratulatory note from him when he learned that I had been inducted into the U.S. Table Tennis Hall of Fame: "Dean, what a great and well-deserved honor. I'm happy to see that all of those hours I put in with you playing ping pong in my basement in 1958 paid off."

Bobby Johnson, 15, Clifton, Wins 2nd Garfield Jeep Derby

Jack Mahlbacher, of Carlstadt, Triumphs
In Special Race Before 1,500 Persons

GARFIELD – Bobby Johnson, 15-year-old Clifton driver, won the second annual jeep derby Saturday before 1500 persons on the Cedar Street hill.

18 Entrants

The contest, staged jointly by the Louis Lombardo Post, Amvets and the Garfield Recreation Committee, drew 18 entrants from Clifton, Rutherford, Ridgefield Park, Saddle River Township, Carlstadt and Garfield.

Johnson's Clifton Special-14 served him well in the trial heats and the final run. Second place went to Robert Hines, 99 Midland Avenue, and Charles Nylander, of Rutherford, placed third. Consolation winners in the approved class were Allen Tich, of Passaic, and William Bernat, of Saddle River Township.

Jack Mahlbacher and his Red Flyer, of Carlstadt, won the special race for cars with ballbearing wheels.

Fifteen cars were entered in the approved class and three in the class listed as ballbearing. Mahlbacher entered the approved class but judges Henry Hartmann School, Superintendent John R. Rozema and Vincent Hartmann ruled his car too heavy and placed it in the special class.

Contestants were eliminated in five three-car heats. Johnson won first heat; Nylander, the second, Hines third; Bernat, fourth Tich, fifth. Hine's car, the, Road Hog,

although it was only a crate with four wheels, gave a good account of itself.

Johnson Gains Speed

Hines' car and Tich's jeep, the Flash, took an early lead in the final run, but the Passaic boy's car started to lag behind when it developed wheel trouble. Johnson passed Hines on the final leg by swerving his car to take advantage of a dip in the road.

Mahlbacher won the special race against, Frank Grohsman in his Comet.

Trophies and awards were donated by the Amvets and the Recreation Committee. Other donors were Andrew "Tabby" Veleber and the city recreation department through Councilman Emil Wall, chairman.

Joseph Molchon, Amvet commander, was the chairman of his group and Henry Hartmann headed the Recreation Committee. Mr. Rozema and Vincent Hartmann were the entry judges; Mrs. Emery Wenzel, Julius Miller, Jr., and Steven Rzudilo, finish line judges; Mr. Wenzel and Nicholas Madana, announcers, Amvet members maintained the spectator lines, Andrew, Simko, city recreation director, assisted in the general arrangements.

I, along with brother Ray and neighbor Don McKievet, all contributed to building the racer. We drew straws to decide who the driver in the race would be. I was the fortunate one to be rewarded with the trophy and the recognition.

The extraordinary nature of this event lies in the fact that it was a harbinger of things to come. As my career unfolded, I increasingly experienced episodes of "good fortune" like this which brought me much in the way of return. Only later in life, looking in the rear-view mirror, do I see clearly and do I believe that I was guided by a lifetime of *Divinely Inspired* events.

Robert Johnson, 15, to Make Pen-and-Ink Hobby Profession

By Marie Hugo
Herald-News Correspondent

Robert Johnson, 15-year-old son of Mr. and Mrs. Dean A. Johnson, 43 Katherine Avenue, Allwood, expects to make his present hobby of pen-and-ink drawing his profession after graduating from Clifton High School, where he is now in his junior year.

Bob, who is taking the scientific course in high school, has already made plans to enter art school in Newark. Since he started to draw when he was eight years old, he has produced many drawings, including portraits of General Douglas MacArthur, the late General George Patton, Secretary of State Marshall, Joe Louis and other prominent figures.

Proud of Ruth Drawing

One of the pictures of which Bob is most proud, hangs in the tavern operated by his grandfather, Michael Donohue, of Martin Avenue in Clifton. The picture shows Babe Ruth when he was the New York Yankees' famed "Sultan-of-Swat". His grandfather is particularly proud, of the picture because he and his brother, James, of Mountain View, are personal friends of "the Babe". Bob has drawn another picture of Babe Ruth showing him leaving the hospital last year after his long illness.

Bob has taken no formal instruction in art, other than the regular grammar school drawing classes. His mother says he becomes more and more devoted to his hobby each year and he now seems to be constantly at work at a drawing.

His interests are not confined to drawing, although it takes much of his time. Last summer he won the Garfield Soap Box Derby and was awarded the first place trophy. He also finds time to help out at Johnson's ice-cream bar, owned by his father and uncle. Bob's paternal grandparents, Mr. and Mrs. Frederick Johnson, are long-time Allwood residents.

FROM BOY'S PEN -- This drawing of Harold J. Adams, principal of Clifton High School, is one of many which have been completed by Robert Johnson, 15-year-old high school student. He is planning a career as an artist.

E ven in my early teens, instincts told me that career choices should not be based on income potential alone. Many Harvard MBA types start on Wall Street or in law firms in the high five-figures; many entertainers and athletes make millions in their teens.

Does that mean that they "have it all" or that we should aspire to a career as a Wall Street broker, a lawyer, entertainer, or athlete because those careers pay well? Not at all—not unless we have a unique talent or passion and a strong work ethic to bring to one of those careers.

Career choices should be based on what you love to do. When you love what you do, you'll never work a day in your life, provided that what you love can lead to a marketable skill for which you will be paid well. You'll have a significant head start in a career if you find early what it is you love to do.

THE BRADY BUNCH

Jack's parents John and Phyllis Brady.

In November 1942, our family relocated—a mere three blocks, from Scoles to Katherie Avenue. As a result of this move, more *Divinely Inspired*, life-altering events began to unfold. Several houses up the street from us lived the Brady family—John, Phyllis, and son Jack.

Seventeen-year-old Dean and Jack Brady in 1949.

Born in April 1929, Jack Brady was three years older than I, but our proximity provided many opportunities for recreation and socializing—ping-pong in their basement, pitching a tennis ball against their front steps, basketball in the lot behind the Serwin house across the street.

While I was still in elementary school in the Allwood section of Clifton, Jack was already attending *Pope Pius High School* in Passaic where he lettered in three sports—baseball (third base), football (fullback) and basketball (guard). He was also president of his senior class!

Jack Brady was brilliant, but he was a paradox. At about 5'6", he was a powerhouse on the athletic field, and I witnessed firsthand how brutal he could be in street fights. At the same time, he had the sensitivity of a fine artist. His pen, ink, and pencil sketches of Franklin Delano Roosevelt, General Douglas McArthur, General George Patton, me from a sitting (below) were masterpieces!

Upon graduation from Pope Pius in 1946, Jack entered the *Newark School of Fine and Industrial Art,* from which he graduated in 1949.

THE GENIUS & TRAGEDY OF LOUIS KNIEP, JR.

Grinds Out Copy in Grist Mill

By STUART H. LOORY
Staff Correspondent.

MILLBROOK—Mr. commuter, you say the subway strike has you beat? Is this the time of year when the dirty, gray slush kicked up by New York City traffic makes you yearn for a job close to home?

Eleven people here don't have those problems, they work in a building nestled alongside a tranquil trout stream in this Randolph Township hamlet, two miles from industrial Dover.

Kniep Associates, an industrial advertising and design agency, is a haven for Madison Avenue refugees housed in a 217-year-old converted gristmill in Grist Mill Rd. off Rt. 10.

The mill also serves as the home of Mr. and Mrs. Lou Kniep and their two children, Kip, 12, and Jerry, 10.

For Kniep it was a case of finding the home first and then going into business.

"I was looking for an old farm or a barn," Kniep said. "I found this little mountain stream and nice old mill and that was for me."

Like Dream House

The dilapidated building Kniep showed his wife, Nancy, for the first time in 1946 was not unlike Mr. Blanding's dream house. It had not been used since 1910 when the last grain was ground. Mill machinery, including the old waterwheel, was still in place.

The Knieps went to work. Soon the interior was transformed into a neat four-room house which they began to fill with early American antiques culled from second-hand stores and auction sales in the area.

Where the waterwheel once turned, Kniep created a studio, hung out a shingle and declared himself in business as an industrial designer far from the city streets.

Work Piled Up

The work began to pile up on his desk and, in 1949, he took on advertising work at the insistence of one old account. Soon an annex was built and today his fulltime staff numbers nine beside himself and Mrs. Kniep, the firm's treasurer.

Edward S. Cooke of Washington Valley Rd., Morris Township, is one contented employe. Since he left New York nine months ago, Cooke, vice president of the firm and an account executive, has been saving three hours a day in commuting time.

His last job was with a New York publishing house and before that he worked for a Madison Ave. advertising agency. Said Cooke: "I have found life much easier and happier here."

Have Swimming Breaks

"We have coffee breaks and when the weather gets warm enough, we have swimming breaks," Kniep explained. When a designing problem gets tough or a slogan just won't come, an employe can let his imagination soar while he casts a fly—in season."

But to show that a feeling of freedom is relative, Kniep feels that New Jersey is getting too overcrowded for him to pursue one of his favorite hobbies, hunting.

"The side of the house got peppered once with buckshot," he said. "During deer season we tie the dogs and kids up," he quipped. "I like hunting but I won't go in New Jersey, I go to Maine where there's some open space."

AT WORK—Kniep consults with John A. Brady over ad layout made in office at mill.

AT HOME—Mr. and Mrs. Louis Kniep Jr. in living room of their former grist

Lou Kniep, Jack and Lou's wife Nancy in 1950.

One of Jack's instructors at the school was Louis Kniep, Jr. Lou owned and operated an ad agency in Dover, New Jersey with his wife Nancy.

Lou must have recognized Jack's talent and work ethic at school, for he hired him immediately upon his graduation from NSFIA.

Jack Brady was a *talent,* but he was all about Jack. He was not one to think about others or share. He suffered, I believe, from "only-child" syndrome.

However, his mother, Phyllis, was just the opposite—she devoted her life to *others.* She was a teacher at *St. Nicholas Catholic School* in Passaic and treated me as one of her children. She was responsible, I believe, for the many times I was invited to join the Brady family on vacations in Cape Cod. I believe Mrs. Brady saw me as Jack's younger brother, and she was a big influence in events that were to follow in my life.

I had some idea of what I wanted to do in my life—perhaps because my interest in doing pencil and pen-and-ink sketches and oil paintings on my own. I enjoyed the recognition it occasionally brought. Fortunately for me, it turned out to be an interest which would lead to a marketable skill.

My plan, upon graduation from high school was to follow Jack's example and enroll in NSFIA. But Jack needed an assistant/intern at the agency, so Jack and Lou Kniep called me to a meeting at the agency in December 1950 and offered me an opportunity I could not refuse. It didn't take much to persuade me to come to work at the agency and go to NSFIA Evening School. By agreeing to their proposal, I set my life on a path that would guide me for the next sixty-five years!

Soon after that meeting, with the promise of a job and with the help of a down payment from my mother, I bought a near-new 1949 Chevrolet coupe for the commute to work. The price of the car was $1,100. In December 1950, I started working for Lou Kniep at $25/week and attending *NSFIA* evening school at $45/semester.

I believe that every piece in my career puzzle, guided, I believe, by *Divine Inspiration,* was fitting together perfectly—live at home with my parents, go to school at night, learn things I needed to know on the job, perform a job with which I felt comfortable and with which I was well suited, make enough to put gas in my car and make car payments and still have some time to spare. At $25/week, the job wasn't one I took for the money; I loved what I was learning in school at night and loved what I was doing on the job during the day.

My first term of employment at Kniep Associates was 1950–1953; my second term, after military service, was 1956–1961. Other than my father at *Johnson's Ice Cream Bar*, Lou Kniep was my first real employer. And like a father, Lou took me under his wing.

Lou was extremely talented—not only in graphics and package design, but in building construction, interior design, landscaping, plumbing, mechanical work, and electrical work.

Starting in 1946, Lou and his wife Nancy did an amazing job of rebuilding a 117-year-old grist mill in Dover, New Jersey into a beautiful home. Building an art studio next to the mill and building a summer home on Meddybemps Island in Maine—you name it, Lou could do it.

The 1950s were a peaceful time for Lou and his family. Here he is with his two sons Kip and Jerry painting scenes on Meddybemps Island while their dog Dutchess relaxes close by. Photo by Dean.

Where the water wheel once turned in the mill, Lou converted the space into a studio where, in 1946, he "hung out his shingle" as an industrial designer. In 1949 Lou started to take on advertising work. This was the year in which he hired Jack Brady as art director. It was on September 6, 1950, that Lou filed for the trade name: *Louis Kniep, Jr. & Associates*.

Short-term, this was a win-win for both Jack and Lou. Jack was also very talented and hard-working. Having Jack in the studio to handle design and production assignments left Lou free to solicit new business and service accounts. Lou's formula seemed to be working; at the time, the *Redbook of Advertising Agencies* listed twenty-six accounts for *Kniep Associates Country Ad Agency.*

Kniep Associates was known as an "industrial ad agency," meaning it specialized in graphic design, advertising, and marketing for industrial manufacturers, as opposed to consumer product companies. Today those agencies are known as "business-to-business."

Sixty-five years after I started at *Kniep Associates*, I was still in the business of "business-to-business" advertising—*a testimony to Lou's genius in narrowing his target market to one that would endure.*

Most of the 1950s were a peaceful time for Lou and his family. But that was destined to change. No one could ever have imagined the tragedies that were to overtake Lou and Nancy Kniep starting in the late 1950s.

Note: For more on *Balance,* see *Formula for a Long and Happy Life* on page 245.

Kniep compound in the 1960s—house, studio (connected by breeze-way) storage building (for his boat) and pool. Aerial photo by Dean.

DRAFTED—A BLESSING IN DISGUISE

In an impulsive move, a few days after my twenty-first birthday in 1953, I drove to California with a friend from Passaic and held a job for a few months as a carpenter's helper.

Although it was expected, I was still stunned by the reality of receiving a draft notice in the mail on July 7, 1953 to report immediately to Ft. Ord, California.

I called my draft board in Paterson and persuaded them to allow me to be drafted from there instead of from California. "If you can be here a week from today, we can make it happen," they said. That was incredibly fortunate. They could just as easily have said, "You left us and went to California, now it's your problem."

I reported on time and began military service on July 10, 1953, just seventeen days before the end of the Korean conflict. This date proved to be very significant post-Army.

Basic Training, Ft. Dix, New Jersey, 1953.

A brief period of processing was followed by sixteen weeks of grueling basic infantry training in Ft. Dix, New Jersey. I found Army basic challenging and even considered applying to officer candidate school, but ultimately decided to try to find ways and places I could be of value to my country other than being an infantryman or a leader of infantrymen in the Army.

I requested a meeting with the recruiting sergeant to discuss Army school options, which would be offered to me if I agreed to serve an additional three years in the *Regular Army.*

The recruiting sergeant handed me a stapled booklet of mimeographed sheets with a listing of all the schools offered by the Army—cook school, maintenance mechanic school, crane operator school, truck driver school—in the seemingly endless list, nothing seemed appropriate for me. At the suggestion of the sergeant, I started again from page 1.

On my second time through the list, bingo! *Photo school* jumped off the page! On November 3, 1953, I was discharged from the U.S. Army and became a "Regular Army" private.

This moment, like so many other events in my journey was, I believe, *Divinely Inspired.* Following were twelve weeks of intense, extremely informative, professional photographic training in Ft. Monmouth, New Jersey.

Celebrating completion of basic training.

Making this decision was the first time I had taken a strong, positive action on my own which resulted in a major change in the course of my life.

Following twelve weeks of photographic training which, post-Army, would serve me well in my career, I volunteered for an additional eight weeks of *leadership* training, which was also in Ft. Monmouth.

I was then faced with the uncertainty of what was to be *the* most important turning point in my life until now—one over which I had absolutely no control. I trembled a bit as I stood in line waiting to read the bulletin board which listed the zone to which each member of my leadership class was being assigned.

The question that haunted me was: would my gamble to give the Army an additional thirty-six months of service in exchange for *photo school* pay off?

Or would I wind up a rifleman in Korea after all?

Call it the *Grace of God* or *Divine Inspiration*, but I was the only member of my *leadership* class to be assigned to Germany! The rest of the class went to Korea where, fortunately for them, the conflict was winding down.

To whomever made that decision somewhere in the bowels of the Army bureaucracy, I owe a lifelong debt of gratitude.

Again, with the greatest of good fortune, I was assigned to a photo lab in a quaint, beautiful town in Germany called Bad Kreuznach.

From the time I arrived in *Bad K* in May 1954 until February 1955, I worked in the photo lab at *Signal Corp* headquarters during which I gained valuable photographic experience for what was to follow, not only in my next Army assignment but during my entire post-Army career!

What I believe to be one *Divinely Inspired* event after another occurred between July 1, 1953 when I was drafted and October 23, 1956 when I was discharged.

Lab skills were among the many things I learned about photography in the Army.

In December 1954, at the suggestion of a fellow in the photo lab named Bob Parker, we took a three-day leave and applied for "Temporary Duty" with the Army Ski Patrol in Garmisch-Partenkirchen, Germany. The mission of the Ski Patrol was to oversee the safety of tourists, particularly those in the military.

Bob Parker in Garmisch-Partenkirchen.

When Parker and I returned to Bad Kreuznach, Mr. Harrell, the Warrant officer in charge of the photo lab said to me, "I won't refuse your request for ski patrol, but if you'll forego it, I'll offer you the option of a one-month 'test' TDY (Temporary Duty) in either Mainz, Mannheim, or Baumholder to be the field photographer there."

However, Mr. Harrell strongly recommended Baumholder be my choice because, he said, "it will offer you many opportunities to practice photography."

"You'll be housed in a Bachelor Officer's Apartment, have your own 4x5 Speed Graphic, your own custom photo lab, as many supplies of film and flash bulbs as you need, a reporter assigned to work with you and you'll have your own jeep. Assignments will come once a week from Headquarters' public relations office." There was no way I could refuse Mr. Harrell's offer.

The calculated risk was paying off! The result was photo lab and photographic experience with over 250 photos published in *Stars and Stripes*, the division newspaper, *Hell on Wheels*, and other publications. Some were sent over the wire services; AP and UP and some even published in *Saturday Evening Post*!

How good, how fortunate, how *Divinely Inspired* was this for me? It was practically an extension of some of what I had been doing at Kniep's and preparation for what I hoped to do when I returned!

After I accepted Mr. Harrell's offer, the "test" TDY extended to twenty-one months. My lifestyle and future were again to be dramatically impacted in a positive way.

September 1954—2nd Armored Division Air Force Section shooting with a 4X5 K-20 camera out the window of an L-19 reconnaissance aircraft.

The one-month TDY, which started in January 1955, extended one month at a time until my rotation back to the States and discharge from the Army in October 1956. This "TDY" provided me with valuable experiences—experiences I could hardly have gained in any other way.

What I believe to be one *Divinely Inspired* event after another including this "TDY" to the training ground in Baumholder, Germany and experiences I gained there have had a lifelong impact on both my personal and professional life. *Never in my wildest dreams did I think that military service could offer the long-term benefits that it did!* The value of the photographic training I received in the Army—not only during photo school in Ft. Monmouth but in my first assignment to the photo lab in Bad Kreuznach, and in the twenty-one-month Temporary Duty assignment in Baumholder—cannot be overstated. At every stage of my sixty-five-year professional career, my experience with a camera and my graphic arts background paid dividends.

My TDY in Baumholder was like our life on earth, "a wisp of smoke." When asked about his life, Fred Johnson said: "so fast by it went." I feel the same way; it's why, at 85, I published the book *How The Years Passed By*. "Quickly" is the answer.

LORI EBER

Lori Eber, a civilian living in Bad Kreuznach, somehow gained permission for easy access to the Army compound called Foch Kaserne. I met him in the recreation hall where a group would meet for relaxation and occasional ping-pong. I played him a few times.

Over time, Lori and I struck up a friendship. He took me for rides around the local area on his motorcycle, took me into his home for dinner with his family, and invited to his sister Evelyn's wedding.

Lori was also the son of the owner of an MG dealership in Bad Kreuznach, Edgar Eber. One day in 1955, Lori mentioned to me casually that his father's dealership had purchased a near-new MG TF 1500. The original owner was an Air Force pilot who had unexpectedly been reassigned to the U.S. I asked Lori what his father was asking for the car. Lori said he would ask him and let me know.

The next day Lori said, "My father will sell it to you for what he paid for it: $U.S. 1,100." We went immediately to the dealership to look at it. It was in pristine condition; the odometer read less than 5,000 miles.

I had already calculated that I could swing it. My Army salary as a PFC was $105/month. With food and clothing supplied by the Army, my expenses were almost zero. I had an allotment of two cartons of cigarettes/ week at $1.00/carton. I didn't smoke so I sold my allotment on the "economy" for 20 German Marks or $5.00/carton for $8.00/week profit—which left me with more than $135.00/month—more than enough to make the payments on the car.

My meeting and friendship with Lori Eber, which I believe was *Divinely Inspired*, provided me with a unique lifestyle and life- altering opportunities during the balance of my time in Germany!

With Lori Eber in 1953.

Post-Army, in my professional life, skills which I learned in the Army worked for me in more ways than I could have imagined. Photography was an entrée to every project for which I was hired; every ad I designed, every brochure, every event required photography.

Entering a project at the photography stage was invaluable; it gave me control of a project from beginning to end—photography, concept, layout, pre-press, and printing. My Army training enabled me to become a "one-stop shop" for my clients.

With very few exceptions, a client never had to call in a professional whose principal income was derived from photography; my time handling the photography for a project was included in production costs.

During my career, there was hardly a photo assignment I couldn't handle with my 35mm camera and a tripod! What a gift I was handed!! How *Divinely Inspired* and how grateful I was for my U.S. Army training and experience!

While in Baumholder, I had more than 250 photos published, some for the AP, UP, and Saturday Evening Post. Every photo, every spread was attributed "Photo by Johnson" from which I gained notoriety. I was always impressed with how eager even generals were to do what I asked them to do. Every time one of them would show up for a photo shoot, they would ask, "Where's Johnson?"

Covering General Maxwell D. Taylor, U.S. Army Chief of Staff, visit to Baumholder on a cold
April 19, 1956. Other celebrities of the time I covered included Francis Cardinal Spellman
and General Anthony ("Nuts") McAuliffe.

Dean's backlighting tanks while the camera sits on a tripod on a hillside with the lens open.

FRIENDSHIPS - PHIL VANCE

Friendships were not something I made easily—not in elementary school nor in high school. Cousin Ken Stewart and neighbor Jack Brady were somewhat "friends," but Ken was part of the family and Jack was three years older than I.

While in high school, I had but one date—with a neighbor named Dorothy Reynics. I never asked her; she asked me. I hardly knew her. She must have been desperate for a date to her school prom to ask me.

Following high school I was part of a crowd that moved from Herm and Lou's luncheonette on Broadway in Passaic to Leo's Bar and Grill across the street. Most of the "crowed" were lovable, Passaic "dese, dems, and dose" guys.

Lennie (The Greek) Paterno, Dean (aka Bob) and Carmine (Manooch) Cresenta.

It was there that Carmine Cresenta said to me one day, "Bobby, you have to get out of this crowd. You can do more with your life. You can say those big words."

Phil Vance, whom I met in the public information office in Bad Kreuznach in 1954, enjoyed many of the privileges I didn't—

relatively well-to-do parents and a good education. But somehow, Phil and I bonded and formed a friendship which would last for almost sixty-five years.

Phil, who was born in Springfield, Illinois, but did post-graduate work at the University of Oslo, was non-standard. He had everyone in the PIO office convinced, including me, that he was Norwegian; he pretended not to understand any instruction he was given with which he did not agree.

Meeting and having Phil as a friend, combined with my Army experiences in Germany, was a great education in itself.

Meeting Phil Vance in Bad Kreuznach and developing a friendship with him was an inspiration, a learning experience, and a sharp contrast to the best friends I had in New Jersey with whom I'm posing on the previous page.

In February 1956, I drove from Baumholder, Germany to Oslo, Norway for a skiing vacation with Phil.

On the way to Oslo, somewhere in Sweden, a tire on the MG blew out on a sub-zero, windswept, lonely road which was beginning to darken. The wheel spinner was frozen to the axle! I honestly believed I would freeze to death on this deserted road trying to remove it—one of several near-death experiences I had in my life. Somehow I managed to hammer the spinner off moments before my hands would have frozen, and I made it to the next town where I found a service station to repair the tire.

The main campus of the *University of Oslo* is located on the western outskirts of the city. Using contacts at the school, Phil arranged for the two of us to stay in one of its dorms. On our first full day there, we took a train to Holmenkollen outside of Oslo. In this photo, we're heading for the trails which will take us to the train back to downtown. Bitter cold, but a "cool," exhilarating experience.

My MG was not a car suited for sub-freezing temperatures in Norway.

Phil and I were prepared for any eventuality that involved travel. Here, parked next to our BOQ (Bachelors Officers Quarters) apartment in 1955 are: Phil's Volkswagen, our Jeep, and my MG-TF1500.

Crossing the Rhine River during September, 1955 "Field Exercise"—just south of Rüdersheim and Bingen. My passenger is Assistant Driver Downing. In the back seat is Jacob, a civilian KP.

Phil as reporter and Dean as photographer doing their jobs at Hell on Wings Airstrip in Baumholder. August 28, 1955.

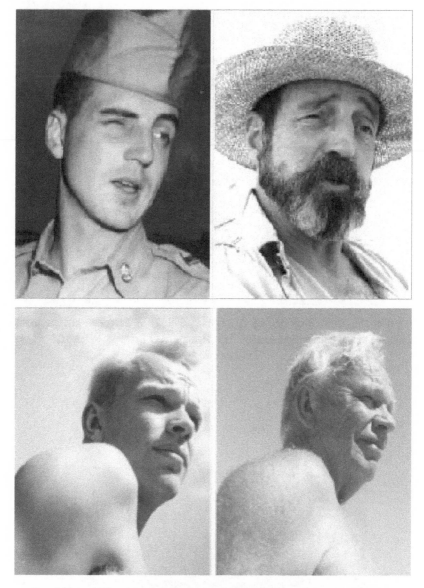

Dean's idea of "Time lapse" photography of friends Phil Vance and Jan Carlsson.
Photos by Dean. How the years passed by.

STRANDED IN SPAIN

During my thirty-month military *tour* in Europe, I had done some traveling, but I decided that one grand tour of areas I had not yet seen would be time well spent.

After spending a day in Rüdesheim with the sister of a fellow with whom I played some ping pong in Baumholder named Marga Fechter, I left Bad Kreuznach and headed to Paris on August 9, 1956.

During the trip I had an extremely unnerving "good news, bad news" experience and a meeting that would change my life forever.

Until August 13, the trip was, for the most part, uneventful—I made Paris in one day and hated it. Traffic was perpetual gridlock, and because of my nonexistent French language skills, it was nearly impossible for me to find anything. It was dark when I arrived; I couldn't ride around all night, so I found a hotel that cost almost as much as I had budgeted for the entire day! I couldn't wait to get out of Paris.

The next morning—August 11—I enjoyed one of the finest and cheapest breakfasts I'd had in any restaurant anywhere—it was at the *American embassy*! Of course I did manage to make a few stops that day—the typical tourist destinations—Eiffel Tower, the Louvre, Champs Elysées, and Pigalle. That night I returned to the embassy for a pork dinner and bought three sandwiches and a jug of red wine for the trip the next day.

After a stop in Bordeaux on the 13th, I had one of the most eventful (and unnerving) days of the trip. It started at 6:00 AM and a short five-mile drive outside of town to an Air Force base for breakfast. Destination Madrid. My first shock was at customs where they charged a $1.25 toll for which I hadn't budgeted.

The drive over the mountains was very difficult; the road was bumpy, winding, and steep. The rest of the road to "here" was not bad. The bad news was, however, that I could not say where "here" was because I had no idea where I was when the MG's engine died!

It was extremely hot that day. *The gas line may have a vapor lock,* I thought. I let the engine cool and tried again to start it, without success.

On-lookers started to gather; they were fascinated by the car. They probably had never seen an MG. I tried asking the locals standing around for the location of a bank where I could cash a Traveler's check. They made it clear to me that the bank was closed. One fellow offered me the equivalent of $15.50 until it opened.

There was not a car in sight in this town so I doubted if anyone would know how to fix an MG. I didn't think things could get worse, but they did! I tried again to start the engine and *it would not even turn over.*

With the help of some of the folks surrounding the car, we pushed it to the garage of a nearby hotel. The owner asked me if I wanted a mechanic to look at the engine. I got across to him that I would like to wait until "mañana" but I didn't know how to explain to him the fact that I wanted to wait until I had some money to pay for repairs. He ignored me and called a mechanic. A mechanic soon arrived. It took him all of fifteen minutes and $.25 in labor to fix whatever the problem was.

By this time, it was too late to continue to Madrid, so I asked for a room in the hotel for the night and got ready for dinner, both of which made me very uneasy. The room they offered smelled musty— the mattress was damp—like it hadn't been slept in or cleaned for years; the room had no running water and the door could be closed but not locked. As I passed by the restaurant in which dinner was to be served, I was shocked to see it swarming with flies! I'd never seen anything like it. But to me, staying here was better than taking a chance on breaking down somewhere in the middle of the night between here and Madrid.

While waiting for dinner—which was to be served at 11:00 PM—the two *mecanicos* that had worked on the car and a couple of other men from the village signaled to me to come with them. I had no choice but to go along with whatever it was they had in mind. They headed out of town, down a very narrow and lonely road. It was starting to get dark, and I was starting to feel anxious.

After about a thirty-minute walk, we approached the side of a hill in which there was an entrance to what looked like a cave. We entered the cave, which was not only pitch dark but cold and damp. I had no idea where I was, or what the folks I was following had in mind for me. I felt more vulnerable than I ever had in my life. I could die here, and no one would ever know what happened to me.

As we walked deeper into the cave, it got a bit brighter from a lantern. I could make out to the left what looked like a wooden drinking trough for animals.

A frail-looking elderly woman seemed to appear out of nowhere, carrying a large jug on her shoulder. It looked like a wine jug and it was. She poured some wine out of the jug, which apparently had been filled from kegs stored further back in the cave, into the trough. It didn't seem to bother her or anyone else that there were flies in the trough many of which were dead and floating in the wine. From the trough, the wine was then ladled into a large glass that had a narrow neck and a funnel-like spout. When the glass was tilted, the wine poured out of the spout and into one's mouth without the glass touching the lips. This vessel was passed around to everyone sitting around the trough, from which we all drank.

After nearly two hours of drinking the "cave wine," on the way back to the hotel, I felt very relieved that my drinking friends had nothing in mind for me other than drinking and, at that point, I was too drunk to care much.

Back at the hotel we all enjoyed dinner, which included an omelet, wine, boiled potatoes and gravy, more wine, pork chops, and more wine. At the hotel were two touring Englishmen. Together we had another six rounds of martinis at $.20/round.

Prior to leaving in the morning, I made my best efforts to pay for the hospitality of these wonderful folks in Spain, to no avail. They would take not one paceta for the hotel room, the meals, the car repair, or the wine.

My next destination, Madrid, was notable again for hospitality. I was already way over budget. I had just $60 in *American Express* checks and $22 in pacetas (880) with seventeen days left on the trip.

The folks with whom I stayed at the *Residencia Arizona* were more than generous; for three days the stay, room, and meals were just $3.75, which included washing and pressing my clothes.

The next day, August 18, I was up at 6:30, had breakfast, rotated the tires and headed for Barcelona. Again, the ride was not easy. It was only 188 miles, but it took nearly six hours. The roads were climbing, twisting and generally rough. The hotel I found in Barcelona—the *Victoria*—was $4 a day with meals. Next destination, Nice!

The trip to Nice was 560 miles and fifteen hours, but it wasn't bad. Good music all the way—some beautiful views going over the Massif des Maures Range of Mountains between Marseille and Nice. I almost ran off the road, however, at the first sight of a young lady in a bikini. I had never seen anything like it in public. That night I stayed in a camping platz ten Ks outside of Nice to make up for the extravagances in Barcelona.

Trousers got soaked helping a crew bring a capsized sailboat ashore following a sudden gale along the French Riviera on August 19, 1956.

JAN CARLSSON

Jan, a traveler from Sweden, was a student on a track scholarship at the University of Michigan in Ann Arbor. He was hitchhiking around Europe with a friend and fellow student named Dick Hill. On this day, a man on a scooter stopped and offered *one of them* a ride into Nice, France. Jan and Dick flipped a coin to determine who would join him on the ride. The coin fell in Jan's favor.

This coin flip on a street on the outskirts of Nice, France would impact *my future for the rest of my life.*

Jan's scooter driver dropped him off near a USO in Nice. Jan walked into the USO just moments before I did. We were both going in for the same reason: free doughnuts and coffee.

While waiting in line, Jan and I struck up a conversation, ate, then played some ping-pong in the recreation area of the USO. I invited Jan to do some sightseeing with me. We started by visiting the beaches in Nice, then Jan joined me on my trip.

The next day we drove to the beach at Cannes, which was mostly sand, not rocks. We found a hotel there for $1 each. I found in Jan a good source for money-saving ideas: finding cheap places to stay, to eat, having cookies and coffee at the USO, and at times, skipping meals.

At the Monte Carlo beach. A rocky beach was something new to me.

Jan was not only a track star at the University of Michigan but, as you can see from the above photo taken the day after he and I met in Nice, an excellent diver as well.

Jan and I try water skiing at Juan le Pin

Since this was my first time water skiing, the serviceman in charge offered a brief lesson for beginners. He explained the process of sitting on the dock holding onto a bar (fastened to the cable connected to the boat) until the boat moved forward and the cable became taut, at which time I was to let myself be pulled off the dock allowing the skis to hit the surface of the water with the tips up.

For some reason, I slipped off the dock prior to the line being taut and found myself standing with my skis in mud in about ten feet of water. I was then faced with the challenge of patiently holding my breath and waiting for the line to become taut. When it did, I had yet another problem—maintaining a grip on the bar against the tremendous force of the water being pushed against my chest as the boat sped forward. Barely able to hold on and keeping the ski tips up, I finally surfaced to see the two servicemen that were piloting the boat laughing hysterically. Jan took this picture as I returned from this near-death experience.

On August 24 Jan and I had planned to go to the pool in Monte Carlo for a change, but entry to the pool was 500 francs, so we went to the free beach, changed, and swam the quarter-mile to the beach that adjoined the pool. I was forced to swim with one hand as I held my camera in the other.

We had a glorious day there, rubbing elbows with the elite, diving, and sunning. On the way back, we used the free bus service that the *Metropole Hotel* had for its guests.

After somewhat uneventful stops in Genoa, Milano, Verona, Lake Garda, Venice, Innsbruck, Schaffenhausen, St. Anton, Liechtenstein, and Zurich, I dropped Jan off in Germany, from where he continued to hitch-hike his way back to Sweden. I continued on my trip and arrived back in Baumholder on August 31.

But this was not the last I would see of Jan Carlsson.

RETURN TO KNIEP'S

In October 1956, I returned to the U.S. and, despite the Army's best efforts to persuade me to re-enlist, I was discharged on the 23rd.

A few days before I left Germany, I received a letter from Jack Brady to assure me that on my return I was welcome back at Kniep's.

Upon my discharge, I found myself again blessed with incredible good fortune. Not only could I return to Kniep's to work, but since my period of service began while the Korean conflict had still technically not ended, I was eligible for GI Benefits *which included tuition-free college.*

One week after I arrived home, I started to work at Kniep's and in early 1957 I entered *Fairleigh Dickinson University* Evening School. I committed to an intense 10-credit/semester schedule. As I did at *Newark School of Art*, I focused only on courses that helped me do my job—to make a contribution. If not taking courses which I disliked, like Statistics and Accounting, meant not having a degree, so be it. I never missed having one.

Knowing exactly what I wanted to do and doing it was more important.

On my return to Kniep's, I learned that a fellow named Glynn Roberts had been hired as Jack's assistant but that Lou had other plans for me.

Since I had not been at Kniep's from February 1953 until October 1956, I had no first-hand knowledge of what had actually gone on then.

Jack Brady and co-worker Glynn Roberts enjoying a poolside lunch at Kniep's in 1956.

Apparently Lou had turned over more and more of the responsibility for servicing accounts to Jack, while Jack had delegated most of his art direction responsibilities to Glynn.

According to Glynn, Lou spent much of his time in Maine and entertaining customers. I experienced first-hand how much Lou loved boating on Lake Meddybemps, picking up customers in his convertible Thunderbird with the top down and taking them to lunch. He'd also entertain others who were not customers but were somewhat famous in their professions like veteran newsman *Paul Underwood*.

Time would prove this strategy to be disastrous for Lou.

FAST RUNNER, FAST TALKER

In December 1956, Jan Carlsson visited the U.S. and stayed at my parents' home in Clifton. He was on his way to Jamestown, New York to take a teaching position. During his stay, I accompanied Jan to New York to visit a teammate of his on the track team at Michigan named Grant Scruggs.

Grant winning a track meet on Traver's Island, New York in 1957. Photo by Dean.

Grant was a quarter-miler and still active in track as a member of the New York Athletic Club.

Once Jan was on his way to Jamestown, Grant and I struck up a friendship. I often accompanied him to training sessions at the Club and drove him to meets in the Metropolitan area. The Club was also a social center for us and we played an occasional game of ping-pong between his training sessions.

As I would learn, Grant Scruggs, by my SOS scale, he was considerably more symbolism than substance, except when it came to running. He could run like a deer.

Jan's visit to Clifton was followed by my trip in August 1958 to Jan's parent's farm, Björka, in Locknevi, Sweden.

On my return from Sweden, expecting my father to pick me up at *Newark Airport*, I was shocked to find Grant waiting for me with a girl I was seeing named Mary Nettum. On this day, I realized Grant Scruggs was not only a fast runner but a *fast talker*.

He had called my mother and somehow talked her out of the keys to my car. He then took a bus to Passaic, New Jersey, found his way to where I lived, picked up my new 1958 Beetle *and used it as a moving van* to help Mary relocate from 89th Street on the Upper West Side where they lived to an apartment in *Little Italy* on the lower east side which Mary had rented. He then used my Beetle for his own transportation until I returned! He had no driver's license. I didn't know that he even knew how to drive a car, never mind a stick-shift Beetle.

I was outraged! But I didn't make a fuss about it; I didn't want to have my mother caught in a dispute between me and Grant. But I believe it turned out to be a blessing. I learned who Grant Scruggs really was.

My relationships with both Grant and Mary was never the same. I stopped seeing Mary sometime in 1959. Mary and Grant were married some time thereafter.

Grant and I crossed paths during the early 1990s when he made a surprise visit to our home in Kinnelon. I have no idea what the visit was all about other than that Grant told me that he was in contact with my friend, Marty Reisman.

The next time I spoke to Marty I asked him what he had heard about Grant. He told me that Grant and Mary had separated because Grant wanted a share of the money she had inherited from her parents and she'd refused.

But before we parted ways, this one-time friend, fast talking snake-oil salesman was responsible for sending my life in an entirely new and positive direction.

MEETING BERNIE BUKIET

One day in April 1957, while browsing in a Manhattan Barnes and Noble with Grant, I heard him call from an aisle or two over: "Hey, Dean, here's a book on table tennis." It was Coleman Clark's *Little Sports Library* book on table tennis, published in 1948. I thumbed through it and came across a chapter: *Thumbnail Sketches*

of the World's Best. There I read with great interest profiles of Sol Schiff, Dick Miles, Lou Pagliaro, and Marty Reisman, all of whom were New Yorkers. I wondered aloud to Grant, "How good do you think these guys are?"

Needless to say, I bought the book for $1.25. At my first opportunity, I was on a mission to seek out where these world-class players played—eager to see what world-class table tennis looked like.

The next day, I returned to the city. I recalled seeing a red neon *Table Tennis* sign in a window on the second floor of a building near Times Square. I went upstairs to a large room of tables but no players. One of the men just hanging out asked me if I wanted to play. I told him I wasn't interested but that I was looking for the place where players by the name of Miles, Schiff, Pagliaro, and Reisman played.

"They play uptown," he said. "You want to go there?" He introduced himself. His name was Paul Moorat. He gave me directions.

I got back in the car and headed from Times Square to 96th Street. Above the door to the basement of a building on the northwest corner of 96th and Broadway was a small sign: *Riverside Table Tennis.* I walked down the few steps to the darkened basement.

Sitting behind a desk just inside the doorway smoking a cigarette was a man in his mid-thirties.

He said to me in a strong Eastern European accent, "You play ping pong?"

"No," I said. "I don't know how to play." I had a feeling his question would involve money, and I had just enough for the next few days to cover gas and tolls. "I Bernie Bukiet. I U.S. champion," he said. "You have big country here, how come you can't find someone beat me?" Bernie was the first real table tennis player I had ever met. He had just returned from South Bend, Indiana where he had won the *U.S. Men's Singles Championship.*

Bernie Bukiet in 1957. The impact of my friendship with Bernie was life-altering.

Bernie had done more in his brief career than just win the U.S Men's. In 1953, he defeated four-time National Champion Lou Pagliaro to win the Canadian National Exhibition (CNE) Open.

In 1954, at thirty-five, Bernie had been picked as a member of the '54 U.S. Team to the London World's. At the Wembley venue, he reached the high point of his career. He got to the quarters of the Men's Singles before losing in four to the winner, Ichiro Ogimura—a result that'd give Bernie, playing with a hard rubber racket to Ichiro's foam bat, a #5 World Ranking.

LOU SETS UP A TABLE FOR TWO

Practicing with Jack, Kniep rec room, 1959

Aware of my growing interest in table tennis, Lou set up a table in the room in his home meant for entertaining and recreation. Lou's thoughtfulness provided an opportunity for practice during lunch hours with a new practice partner—Jack Brady.

By 1958, the tables had turned. Jack could no longer dominate me, let alone beat me playing in a chair as he had in the Brady basement in the 1940s. Between lessons with Mr. Lawrence and playing time in New York, my game was evolving rapidly. But athletic and competitive as he was, Jack also picked up on proper techniques quickly. He soon became a worthy practice partner for me.

The table tennis skills that Jack was developing in Lou's rec room would soon pay off for him *big time* in the business world and would have a long-term positive impact on me and my family forever!

Meanwhile, the lifestyle Lou had created for himself and Nancy and their employees had become too casual to last. As Lou told a *Newark Star Ledger* reporter, "We have coffee breaks, and when the weather gets warm, we have swimming breaks. When a designing problem gets tough or a slogan just won't come, an employee can just let his imagination soar while he takes a dip or casts a fishing fly in the brook behind the house." *SOS! (Symbols Over Substance)*

One day Lou had it with the idealistic "country ad agency" atmosphere he had created. "We've got to start getting more work done around here," he declared. *"We're not running a country club, we're running an ad agency," he said.*

Cracks were starting to appear in Lou's system!

JACK BRADY'S SINISTER PLOT

One seemingly ordinary morning in 1959, while preparing my schedule for the day, I received an ominous intercom call from Lou Kniep. Lou wasted no time in asking, "Where's Jack?"

"I don't know, Lou. It was his turn to drive, and he called last night and said he wasn't coming in today," I said.

"Come down to my office immediately," he said. When I got to his office, Lou was visibly shaken. "I can't reach anyone at any of our customers," he said, "not Jerry Monahan (one of Lou's best friends and best accounts, *A.P. Smith)*, not *McKiernan-Terry* (his best account), not *Taylor-Wharton* (his oldest account). I'll keep trying, but this does not look good," he said. (Turning the business over to Jack—bad move, Lou.)

Jack Brady enjoying the pool on a warm summer afternoon at Kniep's in 1958. No one (including me) knew of the sinister plan that Jack was hatching.

Only a few days passed before Lou had to face the reality that Jack had made off with *every* profitable account Lou had. Lou called me down to his office again. He was crying. "We're out of business," he said. *"After ten years of doing the hard work of building my business, that bastard Jack Brady—"* He broke off to give me a choice. "You can leave and see if you can find something else or you can stay and help me rebuild," he said. I told him in no uncertain terms and without hesitation that I would stay and do what I could to help him rebuild the business.

Lou and I immediately began to research target accounts to call on in Northern New Jersey and to plan for each of us to branch out and start soliciting target companies.

Jack Brady: *Here's to you, Lou, for the ten years of training, employment and opportunity with which you provided me.* This behavior on Jack Brady's part was the most stunning example of his ruthless, self-absorbed attitude that I had witnessed in the twenty years I had known him. As much as she loved her son, his mother would have cried over what he did to Lou Kniep.

Glynn Roberts also stayed on and did an excellent job of servicing the art needs of accounts that Lou and I were able to bring in.

Unfortunately, this was just the first in a series of events that would befall Lou and Nancy Kniep—one of them ending in a tragic loss of lives.

Just about the time that my list of potential clients in North Jersey was becoming exhausted, and what work there was to be done in the art department was being handled by Glynn Roberts, out of the blue, in what was clearly a *Divinely Inspired* event, I was offered a marketing position in a company owned by a fellow named Rogers Case, a table tennis player whom I met at the Cranford, New Jersey club. I left Kniep's for the last time and joined Rogers in August 1961.

Leaping forward—except for occasional visits, Helga and I did not see nor hear much of Nancy and Lou Kniep. When I did talk to Lou, he was always up-beat, but below the surface, as I heard from Glynn Roberts, things were going south. Lou himself was being treated for cancer, his family life was dysfunctional—he was estranged from both of his boys (Kip and Jerry) who had relocated to Tennessee and who were not on speaking terms with each other. Lou's life was seriously out of balance.

It would take more than a "happy hour" for poor Lou to recover.

LOU'S LIFE TAKES A TRAGIC TURN

Lou with our two-year-old son Eric, July 1968. Lou was such a good soul.

December 30, 1985, two friends of Lou and Nancy's, Paul and Mary Underwood, were paying a visit for the holidays. Paul was the last to retire that night and the fire department had determined that he apparently threw a cigarette butt, which had not been extinguished, into the kitchen trash.

Lou was awakened by a smoke alarm at 2:00 AM. He went down to the kitchen to try to extinguish the flames, but they were already too intense, nor could he get back up the stairs. He tried to climb a ladder from the outside to get into the second-floor bedrooms through a window but could not because of the heat and smoke.

THE STAR-LEDGER, T[ue]sday, December 31, 1985

Fire at historic house in Randolph claims veteran newsman and wife

By BILL GANNON and LAWRENCE RAGONESE

A retired foreign correspondent and his wife were killed and another woman was severely burned yesterday when an early-morning electrical fire gutted a 225-year-old Randolph home.

Paul S. Underwood, 70, and his wife Mary, 64, of Columbus, Ohio, were found dead by firemen at the 72 Gristmill Rd. residence shortly after 2 a.m., according to fire officials.

Nancy Kniep, who lived in the historic 18th Century Mott's Hollow gristmill with her husband Paul, was listed in critical condition last night in the burn unit of St. Barnabas Medical Center, Livingston, with burns over 80 percent of her body, according to authorities.

Randolph Deputy Fire Chief Ally Meenan said doctors reported Mrs. Kniep had taken a "turn for the good and will probably make it."

Underwood was a foreign correspondent for the Associated Press and the New York Times from 1948 to 1965, working in London and Eastern Europe during the height of the Cold War.

A professor emeritus of journalism at Ohio State University, he and

his wife had been in Morris County for the holiday season, first visiting their son in Washington Township and then spending time with their longtime friends, the Knieps.

Mrs. Underwood was a regionally known artist and portrait painter who recently worked as a courtroom illustrator for several Ohio television stations.

Fire officials said the probable cause of the blaze was an electrical malfunction in the kitchen, although they have yet to pinpoint the problem.

Kniep was awakened by a smoke alarm at about 2:04 a.m. and ran out the back door of the burning house, tripping a burglar alarm in the process, according to police. When police arrived moments later, they notified the fire department and then, with Kniep's assistance, attempted to climb a ladder to reach a second-floor bedroom, said Meehan.

They were thwarted in their efforts by the intense heat and smoke, according to Meehan, who arrived on the scene with the first contingent of firefighters at 2:11 a.m.

"When we arrived, there were flames coming through the kitchen win-

dow," he said. "We were advised by police to enter the rear of the house because the big front door was bolted with three deadlocks and would have made a tough entry.

"When we got in, we found Mrs. Kniep face down on the living room floor. We found Mr. Underwood in the dining room and Mr. Underwood lying in the upstairs hallway. Apparently, they all tried to get out, but Mr. Kniep was the only one who made it."

All four Randolph fire companies fought the blaze in the sub-freezing temperatures, bringing the fire under control by about 3:55 a.m.

Randolph Mayor George Szatkowski Jr. and other officials visited the scene yesterday, noting their concern for the Knieps, who have been active in Randolph affairs for many years. Kniep is a former member of the planning board, while his wife served on the Randolph Landmarks Committee. Both have been active in township Republican party politics.

"It's a shame, a real tragedy, especially coming during the holiday season," Szatkowski said.

"She knows so much about the township and has been very, very generous in lending her knowledge, leading

Paul S. Underwood
Covered Cold War Europe

historic tours of the area," said a shaken Linda Pawchak, chairwoman of the landmarks committee.

Underwood led a nomadic journalism career, rising from the back pages of the Cincinnati Enquirer to postwar London for the Associated Press, to the front pages of the New York Times as a correspondent assigned to Eastern Europe.

He returned to the Times' New York office in 1964, where after a year as a principal writer for the paper's Week in Review section, he resigned and returned to the Enquirer as a foreign affairs columnist and member of the editorial board.

Born in Rock Ridge, Ohio, he attended Ohio Northern University and the University of Cincinnati. He left college a half-point short of attaining a degree because he refused to take physical education, said Ben Phiegar, a family friend in Washington D.C.

"He had a certain flair to him, both as a journalist and as a human being. He even dressed differently," said Thomas Gephardt, an Enquirer assistant editor, who worked with Underwood for several years.

Wearing an ascot instead of a tie, Underwood seemed to sweep into the Enquirer newsroom, Gephardt recalled yesterday "He was a great journalist" and had a sense of drama about him. He had a lot of friends; he was very engaging and personable," the editor added.

Since 1967, Underwood had been a member of the faculty at Ohio State University's School of Journalism, where he taught foreign affairs reporting and other journalism courses.

Columbus officials said Underwood was active in community affairs, participating in a regional world affairs council that invited speakers and other experts and discussed world affairs.

The couple is survived by two sons, Arthur, 35, of Washington Township, Morris County, and Michael, 42, of Arlington, Va., and a daughter, Sidney, 35, of Columbus, Ohio.

This is the scene of a fatal fire at 72 Gristmill Rd., Randolph

What was thought to be Mary and Paul Underwood were later found dead from smoke inhalation and fire. The person thought to be Nancy was found alive but severely burned. The house was all but gutted.

However, that was not the end of this terrible tragedy.

Three days after the fire, the *Morris County Medical Examiner* reported a case of *mistaken identity*. The female victim in the fire, thought to be Mary Underwood, was Nancy Kniep!

The error was discovered when Mary Underwood, heavily bandaged and sedated, regained consciousness and the nurse caring for her addressed her as "Nancy."

"I'm not Nancy," she said, "I'm Mary."

Lou, of course, went into shock when he heard the news. By this time Nancy's body had been cremated on instructions from the Underwood family.

The day after this awful news, the studio, which was attached to the house by a breeze-way, was set ablaze by a space heater which Lou was using to keep it warm. Most of the building was gutted along with all of his customer artwork and files! This was followed by a fire which gutted his summer home in Maine.

What on earth did this wonderful man do to suffer these horrible events? How could Lou survive the emotional devastation of these multiple tragedies? Through action and perseverance! He spent the next three years rebuilding the house, the studio, and the house in Maine.

My friend and mentor Louis Kniep, Jr. died of cancer on February 1, 1990 at the age of seventy-six.

ROGERS CASE

Rogers Case, whose company I joined in August 1961, was extremely wealthy—a multimillionaire when having a million meant something. He had inherited a company called *Transandean Associates* from his father, Daniel Rogers Case. The company not only *owned* the telephone system in Colombia, South America, but manufactured and marketed telephone line accessories which were designed and patented by his father. When I joined the company and learned of the revenue stream coming in from Colombia (in management fees) and Western Electric (in profits) I was stunned by the numbers.

The association with Rogers suited me perfectly—the business was highly profitable, so the atmosphere and the work schedule at his office in Orange, New Jersey was casual. Rogers paid me nearly twice what I was making at Kniep's, which helped further subsidize my table tennis. The increase in pay allowed me to move out of my parents' home and into a $105/month apartment in the new, luxury *Country Club Towers in Clifton.* It marked the beginning of a new, very different lifestyle for me.

With my parents on their first visit to check out my new apartment. At twenty-nine, I was finally leaving home for the last time.

The timing of my move in September 1961 out of my parents' home and into an apartment marked the beginning of a new life, a new job, and what would soon be a new relationship.

I was the first tenant in the new Country Club Towers in Clifton. My efficiency apartment was $105/month, which I could manage with what I was making with Rogers. I found the solitude and the time to catch up on reading, especially my Bible, very satisfying and relaxing as you can see in the photo at left. Some of the table tennis trophies I was starting to win are on the shelf.

Rogers and I made business trips together, played club matches in Cranford together, went to tournaments together, and, importantly, his luxury apartment on Lexington Avenue in New York allowed us to lead a bachelor's lifestyle on Friday nights and to practice and play at Lawrence's table tennis club on 96th Street and Broadway on the weekend. It all seemed too good to be true—and time would prove that it was.

Raul Gutierrez reviewing shipment numbers with Rogers in July 1963.

Transandean Associates was run by a man named Raul Gutierrez who had worked for Rogers' father in Colombia. He handled both bookkeeping and shipment of the *transposition brackets* and *insulators* from a warehouse close to the office on Main Street in Orange. Rogers' mother Ethel and sister Muriel showed up at the office occasionally but were not involved in running the business in any meaningful way.

Rogers with his Transandean staff in Bogota, Colombia in 1963. To his left is 90-year old Dr. Ferrero, who was a colleague of Guglielmo Marconi, known for his pioneering work on long-distance radio transmission.

Very little was required of either Rogers or me to keep the business running and profitable. The company was essentially a cash cow.

After his mother and sister received their share of the monthly income, Rogers did with the money as he pleased—which meant living in the luxury apartment in Manhattan, buying expensive cars, gambling on the stock market, and making frequent trips to Las Vegas for gaming. My role, I finally realized, was essentially to be his table tennis practice partner and travel companion.

PARADISE TENNIS

Paradise Tennis was a game invented by a man named Huntington Hartford. Rogers and I knew "Hunt" as one of the regulars at Marty Reisman's table tennis club.

Rogers and Dean, Paradise Island, Bahamas, 1963—playing not table tennis but Paradise Tennis, which is played on an oversized table with larger rackets and balls.

One afternoon at the club, overhearing that Rogers and I were going to the Bahamas, Hunt told us about *Paradise Tennis* and suggested we visit *Paradise Island* and give his game a try.

Hunt gave me the name and telephone number of the caretaker of the island to contact; his name was Tom Donohue.

When Rogers and I vacationed in Nassau on the way to Columbia in 1963, I called Tom. He came to the mainland in a small outboard to pick us up, and we spent the day with him and his wife touring the island, which was, but for a few cottages, deserted. We learned from Tom that Huntington Hartford was heir to the A&P supermarket fortune and that he *owned* the Island! Hunt has since sold *Paradise Island* and it has become a major tourist destination in the Bahamas.

For more details about Paradise Tennis, see pages 189–191.

On July 11, 2004, during a trip to Rhode Island to visit friends Erica Peterson and her husband Ray, I contacted Rogers' sister Muriel, who lived in Newport. I invited her to have brunch at the *Viking Hotel*. Rogers' son William happened to be visiting his Aunt Muriel, and he joined us.

During brunch, Muriel told us the story of Rogers' tragic ending:

"Due to an unfortunate set of circumstances, Rogers lost everything. In a desperate move, when he knew I was not at home, he let himself into my house and 'borrowed' my collection of John Singer Sargent paintings. Sometime after that Rogers suffered a 'massive stroke' and died at the wheel of his car," Muriel said. She did not go into detail about the "circumstances" which proved unfortunate for Rogers, but from my experience of working with him for two years, they most likely had to do with: technology eliminating the need for *Transandean* transposition brackets, the acquisition of *Transandean's* telephone system in Colombia by a competitor, treachery of a "friend" who made off with the manufacture of Rogers' brackets and, I believe, most importantly, Rogers getting handed a gift of wealth and squandering it on a reckless lifestyle.

Helga and Dean, Rogers' sister Muriel and his son William, Viking Hotel, Newport Rhode Island, July 11, 2004.

1962 CANADIAN NATIONALS

By 1962, I had made some friends in the table tennis community, less for my ability and level of play than for my continuing interest in and commitment to the sport.

World-class players Sol Schiff and Marty Reisman invited me to play exhibitions with them; Bernie Bukiet and I became friends. Bernie's life was a day-to-day struggle. I occasionally invited him to stay at my apartment in Clifton when he was uncertain about where to stay that night.

In the summer of 1962, Bernie suggested that he and I enter the *Canadian National Table Tennis Championships* held in Toronto each year during the *Canadian National Exposition.* Bernie had reasons for asking me, not the least of which was my 1958 Beetle, which meant transportation for him to Toronto—a 475-mile trip each way.

Because of the costs involved, I was cool to the suggestion for a while; but what Bernie lacked in language skills, he made up for in persistence. Bernie was a survivor; he knew how to get what he needed, which, in this case, was a ride to Toronto and back. Bernie's persistence led to one of the most important *Divinely Inspired* events of my lifetime.

Bernie enjoying a smoke in Dean's Beetle on their way to Toronto.

Bernie and Dean in Toronto in 1962.

THE MONTREAL STAR,

Quebec Entry Bids for Big Titles at CNE Tournament

Three of the top women players competing in the Canadian and International Table Tennis championships at the CNE this weekend, will be Louisa Griffin, Helga   Bultemeier and Denise Hunnius, left to right. The Montrealers will represent Quebec, along with a foursome of top players in the men's ranks.

One of the participants at the *Canadians* was a young player named Helga Bültemeier. She caught my eye immediately. She was not only a very accomplished player but very attractive. I gathered my courage and asked her if she would like to "hit some." Our styles seemed to be compatible—her style more proactive; mine tending a bit more defensive.

We engaged in some small talk—"What's your name, where are you from?" She told me she was living in Montreal but was originally from Hamburg, Germany. When I told her I was from New Jersey, she said, "I have an aunt and uncle living in Nutley; is that close to where you live?"

"It is close, I can *see* Nutley from my apartment. If you ever come to visit them, perhaps we can get together," I said.

"Sure," she said.

Later that day I was sitting alone in the bleacher stands watching matches when something hit me in the back of the head. It was a precision-guided orange peel launched by Helga from several rows up.

To me, this orange peel carried with it a subtle message: *I'm interested enough to talk again.* I bounded up the bleacher seats, sat down next to her and we talked. I suggested that we take a stroll around the fair grounds. She responded, "I have matches today; how about tomorrow?" I agreed; and we spent a good part of the next afternoon together and agreed that we would meet again if she came to New Jersey.

On my next trip to 96th Street, I asked a player named Marty Doss, with whom I had become quite friendly (and whom I knew was from Hamburg) what he knew about Helga. Marty said they were in the juniors together and he didn't know much about her except that "she was always well-dressed and was always with her father." To me, what Marty had to say spoke volumes about Helga.

On October 1, 1962, I was excited to receive a letter from Helga with the news that she was coming to New York City on the weekend of October 6 to visit her aunt and uncle in Nutley, New Jersey. She was driving with friends who were coming to New York to visit friends on *Riverside Drive*, JUST BLOCKS FROM REISMAN'S CLUB!

Stunning! A Divinely Inspired series of events! Bernie persuades me to enter the Canadians; Helga and I meet; Helga informs me that her aunt and uncle live less than five minutes from my apartment in Clifton. Now Helga's coming to visit them and arriving on Saturday, October 6, just blocks from Reisman's Club at a time and place I would probably be in any case! You can't make this up, but Divine Intelligence can!

Marty Doss in 1962. Photo by Mal Anderson.

In December 1962, Helga made a return visit to Germany, during which she and her parents took a ski vacation in Wintersportplatz, Obersdorf.

April 1963

TABLE TENNIS TOPICS

The Official Magazine
of The United States Table Tennis Association

HUNNIUS WINS
SECOND GRAND SLAM

For the second time in two months, Denise Hunnius of Montreal took all three titles of a major table tennis tournament. Playing in the Quebec Open Championships over the weekend, Denise won the Ladies Open over Montreal's Helga Bultemeier 3-1; teamed with Velta Adminis of Toronto to take the Women's Doubles over Betty Tweedy and Helga Bultemeier, Montreal and Guy Germain also of Montreal to win the Mixed Doubles over Torontonians Velta Adminis and Howard Grossman. Those four, along with Ste. Adeles' Ed Schultz and Montreal's Claude Landry were just on Friday named to Canada's National Team which will be going to Prague, Czechoslovakia on April 3. The men's title was won by Elias Solomon of New Jersey over Guy Germain of Montreal.

The Legends retrospective I'm working on at the moment (October 2008) is about a player named Sally Green Prouty. She's 85, living in Florida with her husband of 61 years, Carlton Prouty, 93. They both keep busy entertaining in Senior Centers around Ft. Meyers - she plays the piano, he dances.

They were both table tennis players - she is the only woman to win five National Singles titles – 1940, '41, '42, '43 and '44. One of the historical items I learned from Sally was that Carlton was an excellent player in his own right. When she told me that his picture was on the cover of the January 1934 National Ping Pong Association magazine I asked her to send me a copy of the magazine so I could scan it and use it in her retrospective.

For some mysterious reason Sally also sent an April 1963 issue of Table Tennis Topics magazine. On page 13 of that issue is a report on a tournament in Quebec, Canada in which Helga was runner-up in the Women's to Denise Hunnius. There is no way that Sally could have known that there was a connection between me and the results of that tournament. She does not know Helga nor her maiden name.

In any case, this tournament was a life-altering event for both Helga and me. The winner of the Men's event was a player from my club in New Jersey – Elias Solomon. On his first night back at the club after his trip to Canada, he told me about meeting a stunningly beautiful German player named Helga. I was floored!

After having briefly dated Helga in Toronto in September '62 and in New Jersey when she visited the Hoh family in October '62, she sent a card from Obersdorf, Germany in December 1962 in which she left some doubt about returning to Canada, which was devastating to me. When Solomon told me he saw her in Canada, I was elated and promptly wrote to her and, as they say, the rest is history.

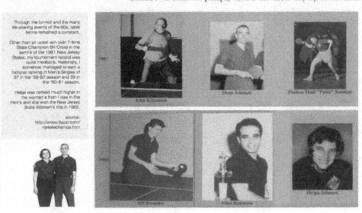

An incredible series of Divinely Inspired, life-altering events.

Over a period of twenty-one months, Helga and I met in Montreal several times, arranged for meetings at tournaments and exchanged correspondence. Here we're on Mt. Royal, Montreal in July 1963.

After numerous 800-mile round-trips to Montreal in my Beetle to visit Helga and a flurry of correspondence, we gathered Helga's belongings and made a final trip to New Jersey on May 30, 1964.

WEDDING DAY

Most blessed day of my life July 25, 1964.

Our marriage, which started with a Divinely Inspired meeting at a table tennis tournament, has lasted more than fifty-five years.

Whenever I'm asked the secret to the longevity of our marriage, I respond:

"There is no simple answer. It starts, I believe, with a *strong common interest* which, in our case, is table tennis and tennis. Add to that a set of common *values*—in Helga's case, European 'old world' values; in my case, values derived from grandparents Anna and Fred Johnson, both of whom had an enormous impact on my upbringing. We share a love and respect for nature, a willingness to work hard, a willingness to work together at achieving a 'balance' and always a willingness to *compromise*. I believe that dealing with marriage issues as a 50/50 partnership is healthy."But keep in mind, men, "a happy wife is a happy life."

When we married, Helga's parents did not know me and I did not know them, but when we met in 1965, Helga's mother and father could not have been more gracious and accepting of me.

During our first visit to Hamburg, they welcomed me with open arms, as did all of the Bültemeier family.

How fortunate, how *Divinely Inspired* it was to become a member of this wonderful family. I felt more fortunate than anyone can imagine. I could not have felt more joy if I had hit the lottery.

The capacity of Helga's parents for giving seemed to be unlimited and their expectations for receiving seemed not to exist.

From 1965, when Helga and I visited Lokstedt together for the first time—to 1969, when Heinrich and Erika visited our home in Kinnelon for the first time—to their last visit to Virginia Beach in 2000 and Helga's last visit to Lokstedt in 2010, many wonderful, exciting visits were exchanged in between.

Helga's parents Erika and Heinrich Bültemeier

Fast-forward to 1973, when I was invited by Heinrich to ski at Türracher Höhe, a
countryside village in the Gurktaler Alps in Austria.

In the winter of 1973, I traveled to Munich, where I met Heinrich,
and we drove 300 km to the *Hochschober Hotel* in *Türracher Höhe*
in Austria.

At the *Hochschober* was a maître d' named Peter. When he
greeted us for our first meal, he expressed his gratitude to us and
said how pleased he was to have us as his guest. Addressing Heinrich
in German, he said, "And we have many nice young ladies for your
American friend."

"He is my son-in-law," replied Heinrich.

One morning, Heinrich pointed to the top of 2,300-meter high
Rinsennoch indicating we were in for a long climb. We took the lift
up as high as it would take us. As I was soon to discover, the boots I
was wearing were designed for ski bindings, not climbing.

Overall, this was the trip of a lifetime and an opportunity to
bond with my father-in-law. However the climb to the top of the
mountain along this icy, narrow ridge you see in the photo on the
next page, there were times when I feared for my life.

Heinrich had been at the top for some time before I was able to
join him. My plastic ski boots had a very narrow base designed to slip
into a ski binding, not climb to the top of a 2,300-meter high mountain.

Following Heinrich's lead along the narrow ridge to the summit, I made it without a mishap. The view from above the clouds was exhilarating.

Following our stay in *Türracher Höhe*, Heinrich accompanied me on a *Sier-Bath* business trip to *Voith Transmissions* in Heidenheim, Germany, where I made a sales call on Werner Simon, the company sales manager. On the return to Ahrensburg, where Erika and Heinrich were living at the time, we also made a stop in Crailsheim to visit a long-time friend of Heinrich's. The return trip, with these two detours, was 800km, which allowed more time to bond with my father-in-law.

MORE THAN ONE PORT IN A STORM

A sluggish economy and, I believe, my relationship with Helga upset my friendship with Rogers. He terminated our business relationship on January 5, 1964.

So the year 1964 began with a mixed blessing; Helga and I were planning to marry, but I was without a job.

With what I was able to put aside while working for Rogers, I made a down payment on this two-family house in Clifton. Toward the end of 1964, Helga and I moved into the downstairs rooms and rented the upstairs to two elderly sisters. This photo was taken in 1967, when Eric was a year old.

On February 4, 1964, in response to an ad in the local newspaper, I was hired for a position in the advertising department of a company called *Raybestos-Manhattan* in neighboring Passaic. The salary was less than I was making with Rogers, but expenses were low. When I accepted the job, I was living at home and commuting was a 10-minute walk.

This month without a job was one of the few times in my life that I was out of work and had to apply for a job. By the Grace of God, every other job opportunity during my 68-year career was *offered* to me.

Being a catalog designer and print buyer at *Raybestos-Manhattan* became tedious and was not very challenging or rewarding either mentally or financially; so I was receptive when one of my suppliers offered me a position. He was an elderly gentleman named John Orr, owner of a commercial photography studio, *The Garraway Company,*.

I left *Raybestos-Manhattan* on March 18, 1966. I was grateful for the opportunity and the experience, but it was a dead-end job.

The pace at Raybestos-Manhattan, while leisurely, was not challenging.

At *Garraway,* I found I'd walked into a hornet's nest when I'd accepted John Orr's offer. Apparently the office manager, Nancy Cook, had been led to believe she would take over the company when John retired. I don't know how she did it, but she wasted no time getting me out.

Less than a month after I started and one month after our first child, Eric, was born on March 5, 1966, I was again without a job. But what a blessing this turned out to be!

A period in my life notable for "mixed blessings" unfolds.

In another event *Divinely Inspired* in its timing and well-suited to my background, John Orr learned of an opening at one of his clients—a company named *American Loose Leaf* in Clifton—a designer and manufacturer of loose-leaf binders. John recommended me for the job. I interviewed with the owner, Mel Schnall, and he hired me on the spot.

By the Grace of God, I didn't miss a beat. Fortuitous in its timing, I replaced a man whom Mel had recently discovered was taking money under the table from suppliers.

The job at *American Loose Leaf* also soon lost its luster, but I was again approached with an opportunity to make a move up— an opportunity I had to seriously consider despite the fact that it was coming from none other than Jack Brady! (That story begins on page 112.)

Executives with whom I worked at American Loose Leaf in 1968: to my right, Jack Mills, on his left a visiting Dictaphone executive and national sales manager, George Schmucki. In 1968 Dictaphone purchased American Loose Leaf from Mel Schnall, the owner who hired me in April, 1966.

In 1969, another *Divinely Inspired* event was sparked by Helga's "uncle" Siegfried Hoh. It turned out to be important to our family in more ways than one. Sig was transferred from his job as a physicist with IT&T in Nutley, New Jersey to Cape Canaveral, Florida.

Sig and his wife Elsa tried renting their home, which they had built in 1964 in Kinnelon, but being "absentee landlords" was not working out for them for a variety of reasons.

Siegfried Hoh was a student-friend of Helga's father, Heinrich. Siegfried's wife, Elsa, was Helga's godmother. Sig died in October 2015 at the age of 100.

During one of our occasional trips from Clifton to Kinnelon to check on the house while it was vacant, Sig met us there and took the opportunity to suggest that we buy it! We willingly and readily accepted.

After a challenging but successful effort to sell the house in Clifton in April 1969, we moved here, to this beautiful, solidly built home, a pond and a barn on six wooded acres in the mountains of New Jersey.

Another year of incredible good fortune and *Divinely Inspired* events was 1969. This was the year in which *Curtiss-Wright Corporation* opened a property they owned in Kinnelon for employee recreation, named *Lake Rickabear,* to Kinnelon residents. *Lake Rickabear,* just a five-minute drive from home, was not only a lake but a gated recreational complex which included walking trails, a putting green, tennis courts, and a clubhouse—all supervised by a wonderful man named Bill Callahan.

Helga and I lived here and enjoyed this home and its surroundings for 25 years.

During the summer months, Helga spent nearly every day at the lake with Eric, Karen, and Kristina—Helga brought their lunches there, they made friends there, they learned to swim there, and we entertained family and friends there.

Helga and Dean at Lake Rickabear in 1971.
Photo by Ray Johnson.

12   Sat., June 25, 1977   Paterson News

Johnson Takes Senior Net Title

Dean Johnson, who played 15 years of competitive table tennis before taking up the full-court game seven years ago, won his first major tennis tournament when he defeated Montvale's Bill Petrusky, 6-3, 6-1, at the Ridgewood Racquet Club Friday to take the Senior Men's Singles Championship of the 47th annual News-Haines Tennis Tournament.

The 45-year-old Kinnelon resident, who qualified for the Senior division for the first time this year, has won club titles in the past, but Friday's victory marks the first non-club tourney in which he has won a championship.

Petrusky said, "I thought I was hitting the ball well and that many of my shots would win me points, but he kept hitting the ball back."

The Johnson-Petrusky finals broke the three-year lock that defending champion Frank Cortelt and Bill Thomson have had on the Senior Men's finals. Cornett and Thomson both forfeited out of this year's tourney.

RICH PELOSI of Fair Lawn will be participating in the Junior Boys' Singles championship round for the second consecutive year on Monday night.

Pelosi, who copped last year's title in that division, earned his way to the finals again by whipping Paterson's Franklin Lewis in straight sets, 6-0, 6-1 Friday evening at the Hawthorne Racquet Club.

"Geez, he was quick," was all a sweating Pelosi could say after beating Lewis in a match that was closer than the final scores would seem to indicate. However, the defending champ's court savvy and versatile repertoire were too much for his opponent.

Pelosi will be facing Chris Chalk, who ousted Greg McManus in a marathon, three-set match that lasted two-and-a-half hours. Chalk dropped the initial set, 4-6, but came back to take the final two sets by identical 7-5 scores.

Ironically, Chalk and McManus are good friends who have played against each other often. The two players have entered The News competition in Junior Boys' Doubles play and will be playing their first match tonight.

Scholastic Boys' Doubles also got under way at Hawthorne with Bill Hoban and Jamie Park defeating Tom Donahue and John Dueh, 6-3, 6-0. Kirk Bachelder and Mike Friedman took a forfeit victory over Jon Salsman and Jeff Samuels.

SENIOR MEN'S SINGLES
Championship
Dean   Johnson   over   Bill   Petrusky,   6-3,   6-1.

ADULT MEN'S SINGLES
Semifinals
Archie   VanVlaanderen over Bill Sarensky, 6-2, 6-1;
Ozzie Pisarri over Gary Summerfield, 6-3, 6-4.

JUNIOR BOYS' SINGLES
Semifinals
Rich Pelosi over Franklin Lewis, 6-0, 6-1; Chris

SCHOLASTIC BOYS DOUBLES
Preliminary Round
Tim Brophy and Jay Pattell over Ron Henke and Len Ricci by forfeit; Gary Simpson and Joe Colombo over Bill Thompson and Matt Lilenthal 6-3, 7-6.

ADULT WOMEN'S DOUBLES
Preliminary Round
Marcia VanTotenbore and Sue Cannella over Kathy McMillan and Barbara Prstek by forfeit.

DEAN JOHNSON . . . News' Senior Champ from Kinnelon

Table tennis experience was an asset for me when I entered, and won, my first tennis tournament in 1977. In my semi-final match I was down 5-2 and match point in the third set but won it in a tie-break.

Sier-Bath engineer and talented artist Larry Trombetta captured my many interests in this caricature he did in 1975.

The most important feature of the lake for our family, however, turned out to be the *tennis courts.*

Many years of table tennis experience taught us fundamentals of "stroke production," how to compete and how to win. We had a "jump" on others who were caught up in the 1970s tennis explosion.

In addition to practicing and competing at *Lake Rickabear,* our playing network extended to *Park Lakes Club* and *Rockaway River Country Club* where we also made friends and competed.

Eric and Karen competing in doubles at Park Lakes Club in 1989.

As Helga and I learned more about the fundamentals of tennis, we taught them to Eric, Karen, and Kristina. All three attended local tennis camps, tennis groups, and, in the summer, *Frank Brennan Tennis* camps.

Eric and Karen had summer jobs as tennis counselors at tennis camps. Karen spent eight summers as a counselor at Carlos Goffi's camp in Florida.

Eric, Karen and Kristina all went on to play college tennis and we became the only family ever to field three teams at the *Equitable Family Tennis Challenge* at the U.S. Open in Flushing Meadow in 1984. We qualified *by winning eight rounds in district and sectional matches.*

Karen has since been coach of the *Middlebury College* women's tennis team and, in 2016, was *men and women's assistant tennis coach* at Pacific University in Portland, Oregon.

All of this was made possible because of the *Divinely Inspired* day in 1969 when Siegfried Hoh asked me and Helga a simple question, "Would you like to buy our house?" When our answer to him was "yes," the direction of the lives of everyone in our family was changed forever.

B12—Daily Record, Northwest N.J. Sunday, August 26, 1984

Family to play in Open

By STEVEN KINNEY
Daily Record Staff Writer

Many area families will get set to make the long, sometimes dull, journey out to the National Tennis Center in Flushing Meadows, N.Y. when the U.S. Open gets under way tomorrow. In fact, many will probably attend more than one day of the nation's most prestigious tennis event.

But regardless of how often they go, chances are no family will enjoy the vantage point that the Johnson family of Kinnelon will, since two members of that family will be playing in the Open — sort of.

Dean Johnson and his daughter Karen, and his wife Helga and son Eric made up two doubles teams, both of which advanced to the national championships of the 10th-annual Equitable Family Tennis Challenge, which will be held at the National Tennis Center Sept. 6 through 8.

Although both Johnson teams reached the national tournament with wins in local competition and the sectional championships, only the team of Eric and Helga will actually compete. Dean injured his ankle during a recent practice, and will not be able to play again until after the Open has been concluded.

That now puts all the pressure of winning a team title on the serves and volleys of Eric and Helga. But that, apparently, is not a major handicap. Johnson feels that his wife and son actually form a stronger team, and Helga agrees.

"I think Eric and I are a stronger combination, but I need all the help I can get," she kidded. "Luckily, I get it."

Indeed she does. And it comes from her son Eric, who played No. 1 sin-

Dean Johnson

gles at Delbarton this past year. He finished the year with an 18-10 record, and was named to the Daily Record All-Area team.

But he never played on Center Court at the U.S. Open, and he now has his first and perhaps last opportunity.

Before that happens, however, he and his mother must defeat 15 other sectional champions in the mother-son division.

If that takes place, it would be the farthest any Johnson team has ever advanced. Last year, Helga and Karen teamed up in the mother-daughter division, but were eliminated in the sectional championships.

"We really enjoyed it (last year)," Helga explained. "We reached the finals of the sectional, so we didn't get a chance in the nationals. But the thing I like about this event is that it's for families, and there are so few tournaments you can enter as a

Karen Johnson

family...especially ones that are fun and where the competition is keen."

And family tennis is a subject in which the Johnson's are fairly well versed.

"With us, tennis is something that happens every day," said Dean, the Johnson patriarch. "With three kids (including 12-year-old Christina) ranked in the Eastern Tennis Association, we have a fairly big commitment to the game."

And what about the Equitable tournament?

"We take the tournament seriuosly from the standpoint that we try hard to win, but mostly we try to have fun."

With two sectional champion doubles titles secured, and a bid for a national championship on the horizon, you can bet the Johnson's have been having quite a bit of fun recently. And there's still more to come.

CBS News sent their sports reporter, Joe Zone, to Kinnelon on September 3, 1986 to interview Kristina and Helga on qualifying for the main draw of the Equitable Family Tennis event at the 1986 U.S. Open in Flushing Meadow.

THE ARNINGS

One fortunate, unintended, but *inspired* consequence of my short tenure at *American Loose Leaf* was being introduced to Maria and Holger Arning.

The shop foreman at *American Loose Leaf* was a man named Bob Green; his wife was in an acting group with Maria's sister. Bob invited us to a 1967 New Year's Eve party at his home in Mountain Lakes, where he introduced us to Maria and Holger.

At the time, Holger was a consultant for *McKinsey & Company*. He impressed us—tall, good-looking, with a slight Norwegian accent, and seemingly knowledgeable about just about everything. Maria also stood out in the crowd—slender with classic features. We heard later that in her twenties, she was crowned *Miss Greece*.

Over time, we kept in touch with the Arnings. Their children, especially Karen and Lisa and Tina, developed lasting friendships; they often exchanged visits between Kinnelon and Cos Cob, Connecticut and we vacationed together at *Pink Perfection* in Kitty Hawk, North Carolina in August 1973.

Our children Eric and Karen with Helga holding Tina Arning by the hand. Kitty Hawk, North Carolina, August 1973.

In the early 1970s, Holger was hired by a company in New York City named *Supradur*—a manufacturer of roofing tiles and siding. His original job description had to do with mergers and acquisitions, but his day-to-day responsibilities included advertising and sales promotion.

In 1972, Holger invited me to his office to discuss his requirements for a wide range of advertising and printed material. By the mid-1970s, *Supradur* was an account second only to *Sier-Bath*.

I had gained a valuable account and our family gained faithful friends because a shop foreman at *American Loose Leaf* invited us to a New Year's Eve party at his home in 1967.

Arnings and Johnsons, triangulated, November 1990. Lisa, Maria, Tina, Kristina, Helga, Holger, Karen, and Dean.

JACK BRADY RE-EMERGES

Since I'd last seen Jack Brady in 1959, he'd established a successful ad agency in Garfield, New Jersey. He came to *American Loose Leaf* in December 1966 under a pretext of needing loose-leaf binders, but his real mission was to discuss a job opportunity with me.

The time was between Christmas and New Year's. Jack came with bad news and good news. The bad news was that his uncle, George Paterson, had died on Christmas Day. George had been Jack's PR guy and helping him with one of his accounts, *Sier-Bath Gear* in North Bergen. The good news (as it turned out) was that Jack offered George's job to me.

Of course, I had reasons not to trust Jack, not the least of which was the way he'd treated Lou Kniep—making off with 100% of Lou's

Jack Brady in 1970.

profitable accounts without uttering a word to anyone, including me—just not showing up for work one day. Bingo! Lou was out of business and I could've been out of a job!

But I also knew that, as he'd done all those years ago, Jack would be doing whatever was in his best interest. If it happened to be also in my best interest, that'd be OK with him. The offer was too good not to consider.

The next day I shared the news about Jack's offer with Mel Schnall. Mel came up with an amazingly creative counter-offer I was comfortable with—to work for Jack part-time and for Mel part-time—and Mel would not reduce my salary if I could keep up with the work!

So my salary would more than double—from $12K/year to $27K/year overnight! Jack's condition was that I (and Helga) interview and be approved by Peter Renzo, *Sier-Bath's* VP of Sales.

After some lengthy discussions with Helga and some soul-searching, I told Jack that I was interested. Jack arranged for a brunch meeting/interview for me and Helga at Peter Renzo's home in Saddle River on Sunday morning, January 1, 1967. (Jack was an *action* guy.)

Peter Renzo at home with his computer in 1970. Peter was ahead of his time.

Peter was not only VP of sales and marketing at *Sier-Bath*—he was the brother-in-law of the president, Ed Bianchi.

The interview was more of a five-star Sunday brunch at the home of Peter and Marilyn—with just Jack, his wife Florence, me, and Helga. Peter and Marilyn liked me, but they *loved* Helga—not only her good looks ("She looks just like Marlene Schmidt, 1961 Miss Universe," Marilyn said) but the fact that she was a table tennis player and that she and I met at a tournament impressed Marilyn.

Jack Brady, in introducing me and Helga to Peter Renzo in 1967, set in motion an entirely new *Divinely Inspired* career for me as he had when he had introduced me to Lou Kniep in 1950.

In seventeen years, life had come full circle, with a third life-altering event—all of which can be traced directly back to three inspired relocations—to Scoles Avenue in 1935, to Katherine Avenue in 1942, and to Ricker Road in 1961.

During brunch, Marilyn casually mentioned that their niece, Terry Bianchi, had recently married a tennis pro from Upper Saddle River.

The comment slipped right by me, but Helga picked up on it immediately. "Are you the family that Frank Brennan married into?"

"Yes," said Peter, "we're part of the Bianchi family. I'm the brother of the wife of Ed Bianchi, president of *Sier-Bath*. Terry is his daughter."

Peter and his daughter, Jeanne, in 1972.

Helga knew of the connection because Frank's mother, Lillian Brennan had invited my mother to the wedding and my mother had shared details of the event with Helga. How *Divinely Inspired* was that connection!

In July 1971, Peter called me at my office at *JA Brady* when Jack was vacationing on Long Beach Island to inform me that there was some "unhappiness" with Jack's billing practices. He said he would talk to Jack about it when he returned, but he wanted to know if I would be receptive to the idea of joining *Sier-Bath* full-time as their advertising manager.

This phone call was a *Divinely Inspired*, life-altering event.

Realizing Jack was about to lose the account, I agreed on the spot to Peter's offer.

My first assignment for Peter and *Sier-Bath* was to assist with an ASME event in May 1967 called the *Spring Round-up*, an annual get-together of about 1,000 executives of engineering companies. An article in *Mechanical Engineering* magazine on page 116 reports on the event.

Terry and Frank Brennan in 1969 and in 1998. How the years passed by. Photos by Dean

The day after I was hired by Pete Renzo, with his permission, I collected the files I needed to do my job as ad manager. The files were owned by Sier-Bath and I was now an employee of the Company. I really had no choice in the matter since Jack was about to lose the account and, again, I would have been out of a job. This move was a bit unconventional, but as I learned as a pre-teen from the Dugan truck driver, "I'd rather ask forgiveness than permission."

ANNUAL SPRING ROUNDUP

Dr. Wernher von Braun
Receives "Man of the Year"
Award From ASME
Metropolitan Section

WITH MORE than 1000 ASME members and guests in attendance, the Met Section came up with a star-studded dinner program on May 11, at the New York Hilton Hotel. Wernher von Braun, director of NASA's George C. Marshall Space Flight Center in Huntsville, Ala., was presented the Section's "Man of the Year" Award for his continuing efforts to advance man's knowledge of the universe, for promoting cooperation in the peaceful use of outer space, and for his skillful, technical, and administrative leadership in guiding U. S. space programs. Outstanding Leadership Awards were also presented to our own Maxine Barends, News Editor, ASME, for outstanding journalism; and to Lester R. Bittel, Charles C. Bonin, Peter Corradi, George F. Habach, Austen N. Heller, Kenneth S. Landauer, J. Eliot McCormack, E. Joseph Sharkey, James F. Young, and Harry P. Vickers.

William Byrne, Past-President ASME and President, Bilbyrne Corp., served as toastmaster.

DR. VON BRAUN displays award scroll which he received from ASME President James Harlow. NBC TV's Lou Wood interviews Dr. von Braun during reception. OUTSTANDING JOURNALISM AWARD is presented to Maxine Barends by Marlene Schmidt, former "Miss Universe." A member of the ASME, Miss Schmidt is a public relations consultant to Sier-Bath Gear Co.

At reception, Dr. von Braun chats with Dean Johnson and Peter Renzo of Sier-Bath.

VON BRAUN   HARLOW

WOOD   VON BRAUN   BARENDS   SCHMIDT

VON BRAUN   JOHNSON   RENZO

In the lower panel of this July 1967 issue of Mechanical Engineering magazine are: Dr. Wernher von Braun, me and Peter Renzo. (In an ironic twist, in a conversation with Dr. von Braun, he confirmed to me that he and Sig Hoh were former colleagues.) In the middle panel is 1961 Miss Universe Marlene Schmidt, with whom I, as photographer/reporter, visited Sier-Bath customers throughout New England, promoting Sier-Bath products. In addition to being Miss Universe, Ms Schmidt had a degree in mechanical engineering.

THE SIER-BATH PATH

I started full-time with *Sier-Bath* on August 16, 1971. In addition to working with Peter, I worked with an Army Reserve Colonial named Howard Giebel, Peter's marketing manager.

I learned early that Peter was a table tennis fan, but I learned only later how a *Divinely Inspired* event played a role in Jack winning the *Sier-Bath* account.

The level of table tennis Jack reached when he and I were playing every lunch hour at Kniep's not only earned him a position on the *Passaic Knights of Columbus* table tennis team but soon made him their best player.

It was here that Jack met a *Sier-Bath* employee named Bruno Dorski. Bruno introduced Jack to Peter Renzo, who, at the time, happened to be looking for an ad agency.

My mind continues to be drawn back to the flip of the a coin on a road on the outskirts of Nice, France in 1956 and my many connections to table tennis, dating back to ping-pong in the Brady family basement in the 1940s.

Following a long illness, Jack Brady died on December 26, 2005 at the age of 76.

Not long after joining Sier-Bath, I found myself embroiled in a dispute between Peter and his twenty-nine-year-old nephew, Clem, Ed Bianchi's son. Ed, as we've learned, was president of the company and son of the founder Clementi Bianchi.

Ed had named Clem his potential successor, and one of Clem's first missions seemed to be to downplay Peter's role in the company. The situation created a stressful environment for me.

Both Clem and Peter began

giving me conflicting assignments. My loyalty was to Peter, but Clem claimed he was acting on his father's behalf.

This dispute was a lose-lose for me. And in early 1974, Clem made me an offer to help him set up an ad agency, taking with me the *Sier-Bath Gear* account for starters. I found it to be another offer I couldn't refuse.

Three generations of Bianchis—Clem (standing) with his father Ed. Portrait of Clemente, founder of Sier-Bath, hangs in Ed's office. Photo by Dean in 1970.

On January 21, 1974 (my forty-second birthday), CJ Bianchi and his accountant Gerry von Dohlen recommended I go off-salary to reduce expenses at Sier-Bath. At the same time, Peter Renzo told me that he needed some work done for *Creative Logic*, a Sier-Bath subsidiary company he founded in Paramus, New Jersey. So an agency was formed to service Sier-Bath's advertising, printing, and promotional needs—and another series of *Divinely Inspired* events begins to unfold!

The details of Clem's offer to head up this new agency was a $2,000/ month retainer plus a normal commission on ad placement and printing.

Clem also offered to introduce me to two of his friends and potential clients; Joe Murphy, a realtor, and Frank Brennan, (yes, *the* Frank Brennan) owner of a Tennis Camp—both of whom needed advertising.

In 1972, my first assignment for Joe Murphy was to produce a promotional folder which featured his entire staff at the time, including his mother (behind him and to his left). Joe's staff eventually grew into hundreds, and his sales of homes in Bergen County grew into hundreds of millions.

In 1972, including *Sier-Bath Gear*, the agency's client list numbered four—*Murphy Realty* and the two Brennan tennis camps. In a paradoxical twist, although Clem had recommended me to both Frank Brennan Sr. and Jr. to handle their advertising, the Brennans had been family friends since the 1930s when Lillian (Coates) Brennan was a next-door neighbor of ours on Scoles Avenue in Clifton.

All the Brennan camps that we promoted were successful, with the exception of Jeff Brennan's. Our advertising did the job for Jeff, but he failed to follow the business model established by his father and brother.

When the campers showed up for Jeff's camp in the summer of 1974, Jeff was nowhere to be found. My understanding was that he had chosen to take some time off to go on a Windjammer cruise with his girlfriend!

Jeff made many promises to pay us for the ads we placed for him in the *New York Times*, but for whatever reason he was unable to follow through. His parents, Lillian and Frank, must have been terribly embarrassed, but in fairness to Frank, Sr., he proactively disclaimed any financial responsibility for his son, Jeff.

On a fateful day in 1974, I arrived at our office in Ho-Ho-Kus to learn from Clem that his right-hand man Maurice (Moe) Paquin, had died that morning. Moe had just flown in on a "red-eye" from California.

When Clem and his father, Ed, and I set up the agency, we rented office space in Ho-Ho-Kus, New Jersey. The space was also shared by another company set up by Clem called *Sierco*—a Sier-Bath "companion company" established to market power transmission products—mainly *Sier-Bath* couplings and gear boxes.

In addition, the plan was to market products for two European Mechanical Power Transmission manufacturers with whom Moe and Clem had made contact—a company called *Voith Transmisions* and another named *Hansen Transmissions*.

In addition to Moe, Bob Miller, Sier-Bath's coupling sales manager was involved with *Sierco* to help market the coupling line. I remember thinking at the time that the structure Clem was creating was fragile.

Feeling some uneasiness about how things might unfold with the way I saw things at *Sier-Bath and Sierco*, I applied for a trade name *Dean Johnson and Associates*—a "fallback" position for me in case Clem's business model did not work out.

Clem, in a clever move, hired a contact he had at Aero-Jet General named Bob Humphrey to replace Moe. Part of Bob's job description was to conclude negotiations with *Hansen Transmissions*, which Clem and Moe had begun and which were intended to assign *Sier-Bath/Sierco* as an exclusive agent for *Hansen* Gear Boxes in the U.S.

But without Moe, Clem procrastinated. As a result, both *Hansen* and Bob Humphrey lost patience.

Bob then contacted Jacques van Heeren at *Hansen* in Belgium directly. They reached an agreement on establishing a Hansen subsidiary in the U.S., and Bob tendered his resignation at Sier-Bath. Shortly thereafter, he opened a *Hansen* sales office and small assembly facility on Main Street in Branford, Connecticut.

Clem Bianchi and Bob Humphrey at a PTDA (Power Transmission Distributors Association) meeting in Chicago in 1973.

On January 15, 1975, not long after the opening of his new facility, Bob called me in to discuss an ad program which included design and production of a new catalog, a campaign of advertising and a series of "application-oriented" brochures. *Hansen* eventually became a major account!

Bob Humphrey and I worked together for more than seven years. *Hansen* sales increased from zero to nearly $8 million/year.

However, this was also not meant to last. According to Bob, one of his "trusted" employees, a Belgian, did him in by indiscreetly reporting some of Bob's business practices to Belgium about which he knew they would not approve. It was rumored that the Belgian had hoped to replace Bob.

Bob called me one day in 1982, in tears, to say that he had been fired by Jacques van Heeren. Douglas Newton, president of *Hansen, Canada* was named to replace him.

Not the last of Hansen. Leaping ahead twenty-seven years, in an ironic twist, in 2009, *Hansen* again be-came a major account for me when friend Marcelo Zapatero became president of *Hansen Transmissions*. He immediately assigned to me all of the company's sales promotion—trade magazine advertising, catalog and brochure production, and trade show support.

Marcelo Zapatero.

Bill Dolwick with his self-portrait. January 25, 1971. Photo by Dean.

BILL DOLWICK—WORLD FAMOUS PORTRAIT ARTIST

In the early 1970s I had a client named *Associated Pile*—a manufacturer of point protectors for use on pile drivers.

During a routine call at *Associated,* the vice-president, Jack Dougherty, with whom I had been working, asked me if I knew anyone who was a portrait artist. A fellow table tennis player at my club named Bill Dolwick came to mind. I did not know Bill well at the time, but I had heard that he was an artist.

Dean's continuing friendship with Bill Dolwick led Bill to offering to do a portrait of Dean and Helga. That portrait, which he did in 1973, from a sitting, proudly hangs in Dean and Helga's bedroom to this day.

During my next practice session in Fair Lawn, I asked Bill if he would like to "hit a few." Following our hitting session, I told Bill that I had heard he was an artist and asked him what his specialty was. He said *portraits*. Bingo!

I told Bill that a client of mine, Jack Dougherty, vice-president of a company in Clifton, was looking for a portrait artist and I asked him if he would be interested in talking to him. Bill said he would. I gave Bill Jack's contact info and he and Jack got together to discuss Jack's needs.

During our next practice session, I learned from Bill that Jack was interested in a portrait of his father-in-law. Jack gathered for Bill a selection of old photos of his father-in-law from which Bill could be guided to create the portrait.

I later learned that Bill had attended the *Cleveland Institute of Art* where he received the *Gotwalt Scholarship* for a painting of his grandfather. He matriculated at the *Slade School of Art* for two years. When he returned from England, he envisioned selling his portraits but didn't sell enough to make a living, so he became an illustrator and worked for *Illustration House*, a company in New York. His paintings became legendary. After several years he was elected into the *New York Society of Illustrators* and remained a member until his death in 1993.

Bottom line, Jack and his family were so pleased with the result that, according to Bill, Jack ordered paintings for several other members of his family.

Bill then offered to do a portrait of me and Helga.

Interestingly, for our portrait, Bill apparently used a technique for creating a painting of photographic quality with just a paint brush such as the artist Johannes Vermeer did in the mid-1600s.

To create the astonishing effects of light and shadow, Vermeer used a *camera obscura*—a box with a hole in it. The inside of the box was painted white and, using a series of lenses and mirrors. it reflected the outside image within. This intensified the light and shadows of the reflection, allowing Vermeer to see finer detail of proportions.

Helga and I sat for Bill as he photographed us with a white background, studio lighting, a 2-1/4 X 2-1/4 Rolleiflex camera, and black-and-white film. He called us again to his studio to give us a choice of views from his proofs.

I was not there to witness first-hand his next step, but I assume he selected the negative from the print we all approved, converted it to a positive transparency, and projected the image onto his canvas to guide his brush strokes.

Ten years earlier, I instinctively used basically the same technique as Bill did—and tools with which I was familiar (photography and a #2 pencil) to create this series of sketches of table tennis legends Dick Miles, Marty Reisman, and Erwin Klein.

NORDSTJERNAN SVEA (50¢)

Nordstjernan-Svea Helped Per Janvid Find N. J. Kin

Per playing the organ at the Svenska Kyrkan in New York on Easter Sunday, 1980.

UNVEILING JOHNSON FAMILY HISTORY

Per Janvid, a second cousin on my father's side, is featured here because he has had such a profound impact on the Johnson family—on family history, genealogy, and in establishing a connection to relatives in Sweden.

In 1979, the Swedish-American newspaper *Nordstjernan Svea* printed a story about Per's efforts to locate his American relatives, whom he thought might be living somewhere in New Jersey. Per, whose home was in Karlstad, Sweden, was working in New York at the time as an assistant to Kurt Waldheim, Secretary General of the *United Nations*. He had with him a copy of a letter which was written to his grandfather Algot from Algot's brother Fred Johnson.

The letter was sent on April 4, 1926 from Passaic, New Jersey. It included enough details to alert a reader of the *Nordstjernan Svea* to the identity and location of the family for whom Per was searching. By the *Grace of God* and the woman's thoughtfulness and generosity, she contacted Per.

Several members of the Johnson family gathered at the home of Floyd and Rose Johnson on January 26, 1980 to meet Per Janvid and to learn of their relatives in Sweden. (l-r) Dean R., Per Janvid, Dean A., Victor, Floyd, Rose, Helen, and Mary Johnson.

On January 26, 1980, Per boarded a bus from New York to
Clifton, New Jersey to the home of Floyd Johnson, son of Fred
Johnson. Floyd's home was directly across the street from the home
which Fred had built in the 1900s. *Even before he debarked the bus,
Per knew, by the similarity in style to Algot's home in Sweden, that he
had arrived at the right place!*

This is an English translation of the letter that Fred Johnson sent to his brother Algot in Sweden. It was this letter that led Algot's grandson, Per Janvid, to seek out the American side of the family and to open up the Johnson ancestral tree in Sweden. Because of the name change on the Swedish side from Jansson to Janvid, tracing the family tree from here would have been virtually impossible.

Dear Brother:

I received your letter of 4 February that is on your birthday, so it is two months ago. I have been thinking of writing to you several times but always something has come in between and that's the way it is when there is nothing new to write about.

Everything is as usual. Today is Easter. The sun is shining. The weather is beautiful but it is windy. Last night there was thunder with a shower of hail. Winter has been pretty good. It has not been particularly cold but that's a good thing because there has been a coal shortage because there was a strike in all the coal mines. But last year we bought coal so we had enough for the whole winter. And in the wool factories here in Passaic they have been on strike for over 2 months but they think it will be over this week. There are about 15,000 workers in these factories.

You also mentioned that your son changed his mind so that he is not coming to America. But you know there is no land as good as America.

In the construction business, the pay is good. The carpenters now get $11.20/day, the plumber $12.00 and the masons $14.00 a day.

Our third son is now a trained carpenter. He will be twenty-one on the 10th of May. We now have only one son who is going to school. He will be 12 on the 6th of August. His name is Victor Adolph.

I should mention a little about the family. We are all well. We have, all of us, excellent health. I have hardly been sick at all since I left home. In 1915 I had a sore throat for one week. I have been working in the same foundry for 24 years and I have only lost that week.

I want to end this letter by extending our best greetings to all of you and I thank you very much for your letter.

Kind regards,
Your brother,
Mr. Fred Johnson
RD 1, Passaic, New Jersey, USA

A LIFE-CHANGING INTRODUCTION

On Tuesday, August 30, 1983, after arriving home late the night before from a family camping vacation in Cape Cod, I received a 7:30 AM call from Douglas Newton, president of *Hansen Transmissions* in Branford, Connecticut. Newton got right to the point.

He wanted to know if I was available to have lunch with him and a man named Bill Lechler, his new marketing manager. The call caught me off guard because I hadn't heard from Newton since he became president of *Hansen*. Newton lived in Canada and I knew that he had his own agency in Montreal. Nevertheless, following my rule of "just show up," I said I was available and I was on the road before 8:30 AM for the 102-mile trip.

Following a short meeting in the *Hansen* conference room, Doug Newton, Bill Lechler and I went to lunch at the *Chowder Pot*.

Back at the office, Bill and I had an in-depth meeting, during which I agreed to propose an advertising and trade show program for the balance of 1983 and for FY '84.

On the following Friday, I mailed a package to Bill Lechler containing the proposal. I later learned that when Bill reviewed my proposal and budget with Newton, he was told that "there would be no money for advertising and trade shows, that you're hired to use your contacts and network in the power transmission industry and go out on the road and bring in orders." That led to a confrontation between Newton and Bill, and Bill was terminated—less than a year after he was hired.

When I called Bill to follow up on my proposal, Linda Ceruzzi, the receptionist, told me that Bill was no longer with the company. I was shocked, and knowing that Newton had his own agency in Montreal, I pursued the issue no further.

However, this was not to be the end of my connection to Bill Lechler. Destiny was not to be denied!

On July 2, 1984, during a meeting with Peter Renzo at his office in North Bergen, Peter mentioned to me that two representatives of *ESCO Power* (Sier-Bath's agent for couplings in Europe) Yves van Delft and Jean Delpire, would be coming in on July 12th to discuss the marketing of *Variable Speed Drives* in the U.S.

Peter had experience with Sier-Bath gears, gear couplings and open gearing but not with variable speed drives. Peter asked me if I knew anyone in the industry who might shed some light on this segment of the PT industry for him. Bill Lechler's name immediately came to mind, and I mentioned him to Peter; he asked me if I knew how to get in touch with him. I looked in my wallet and lo-and-behold, I still had Bill's business card, which contained his home telephone number in Blue Bell, Pennsylvania. How this call unfolded was *Divinely Inspired!* I dialed the number from Peter's telephone and Bill's wife, Jane answered. I introduced myself and asked to speak to Bill.

Not sure if he would remember me from our meeting at *Hansen* a year earlier, I reintroduced myself, introduced Peter and told him that Peter was interested in talking to him about Variable Speed Drives marketing. Peter suggested to Bill that he come to North Bergen for a meeting. Bingo!

To help Bill become familiar with the Sier-Bath product line, I gathered a set of literature—Sier-Bath history and printed material—for him to study for the meeting. Helga and I then met him (and his mother) on Sunday, July 8 at our Country Club in Mountain Lakes.

At the meeting at *Loews Glenpointe* in Teaneck on July 12th, 1984 Bill made a presentation on the U.S. *Variable Speed Drives* market to Yves van Delft and Jean Delpire.

Bill then had a follow-up meetting with Peter and me, during which he presented an invoice to Peter for his services. Peter grimaced a bit at the amount. He handed the invoice to me and said, "sign this and put it in for payment." Peter congratulated Bill on his presentation, they shook hands and Bill left.

I believe Bill never forgot this meeting on this day.

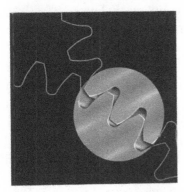

PRECISION GEARS · GEAR SYSTEMS

Among the items that I brought to Bill was one I produced for Sier-Bath in 1968—an award-winning, fifty-two-page, four-color hardbound catalog on Gears and Gear Systems.

It appeared for the second time that my association with Bill Lechler would end, but for a second time I was wrong.

On November 14th, 1984, at the suggestion of Peter, I accompanied him, his coupling sales manager Peter Bennett, and his open gearing sales manager Mike Radoslovich to a *PTDA* meeting in New Orleans.

As we entered the lobby to register, the first person we happened upon was none other than *Bill Lechler! I have no doubt that this meeting on this day in this place was Divinely Inspired!*

Bill told me that he had just been hired by a company "in your neighborhood," *Sumitomo Machinery*; and he invited me up to his hospitality suite. I wasted no time in taking him up on his invitation. His wife, Jane, was his gracious hostess.

Bill had a display of *Sumitomo* catalogs, which he showed to me with the comment, "They look to me like they could use some improving. Call me for an appointment when you get back to New Jersey. I'll show you the plant and we can talk about catalogs." *This was a Divinely Inspired moment that would change the lives of our family in a profound way.*

Dean and Bill Lechler.

On Thursday, December 13th, 1984, I took Bill up on his invitation to visit him at *Sumitomo* in Teterboro.

Following a brief meeting with Bill, he suggested that I work through his advertising manager, Paul Pisano. I immediately called Paul and made an appointment for the next day.

We met in a small conference room off the lobby, and for about an hour, I showed Paul samples of work I'd done, mainly for clients in the Power Transmission industry—*Sier-Bath, Hansen Transmissions, Voith Transmissions, and Torrington Bearing.*

Paul appeared to listen but didn't ask any questions. When I was finished with my presentation he said, "We really don't do that much advertising [only, as I learned later, about $750,000/year]. If we need something, I'll call you." With that, he showed me to the door.

Walking to my car I thought, *Pisano's not getting away with blowing me off like this.* I returned to the lobby and told the receptionist I wanted to speak with Mr. Lechler. She got Bill on the phone and I said to him, "I just had a meeting with Pisano and he blew me off. If it's his decision about whether or not I have an opportunity at *Sumitomo*, I don't have a prayer."

Bill said, "Tell the receptionist to bring you into my office."

To make a long story bearable, several months later, Bill gave Pisano an "opportunity" to work in sales. Then Bill and his office manager, John Cali, who was coordinating printing through *Thompson Printing* and their salesman Jerry Bond, asked me to quote on every catalog job that came up. Bill terminated his relationship with Sumitomo's New York ad agency and asked me to take over the $500,000 ad program. *The Rubicon had been crossed. Life would never be the same.*

Thanks to the good fortune of acquiring the Sumitomo account in early 1985 and the support of Bill Lechler, by the end of the year our billings increased from less than $200,000/year to over $1,000,000!

DEAN JOHNSON & ASSOCIATES

After working out of our home for more than two years, on April 17, 1975, we relocated our agency, along with *Photo Design*, to an office building at 1250 Rt. 23 owned by friend Bob Ward. Bob operated an ad agency and printer in the building named *Carelli, Glynn, & Ward.*

As good fortune and *Divine Intelligence* would have it, I found at *Carelli, Glynn, & Ward* not only an excellent facility and compatible work environment, but three extremely talented and hard-working graphic artists who would eventually become colleagues and friends of mine and Helga's—John and Mary Weber and Les Scott.

Mary and John Weber

In 1975, Mary and Les were employees of *CG&W.* In August of that year, I needed a slide presentation for *Sier-Bath* and I brought the job to CG&W to produce for me. I first reviewed the project with Bob Ward and his art director, Victor Jaskot. Victor then assigned the project to Les Scott for layout of the slides and to Mary for typesetting.

My first contact with Mary was related to that project. In August 1975, I reviewed proofs of the slides with her. Slide production then had to be created on "172 boards" with overlays for color, then photographed with a 35mm camera.

Mary setting type on her new, modern keyboard.

Later that year, Mary dropped in at my office to tell me that she was going into her own business and was looking for space from which to service her customers. I immediately offered her desk space and gave her one of her first jobs under the name of *Type 'N Graphics*—the 1976 *ASME Spring Round-up* seating list, which she typed on her IBM MTST typesetter.

The entire staff of *Dean Johnson & Associates* at this time consisted of Helga (part-time) and me. All others were freelance.

Our agency could not have functioned without Helga.

Helga exhibited persistence and skill as bookkeeper, media director, bill collector and master of the *Atlee Brown's Ad Agency computer system*. Atlee's system was difficult for her at first but she stuck with it and, over time, mastered it—all in addition to raising three children, running a household, cooking and gardening, making time for her own tennis, and helping the kids with theirs, all of which allowed me the freedom to concentrate on servicing customers and coordinating the activities of Mary, John, Les, and Ray.

Soon after moving to the CG&W building, I began giving business to Bob Ward's *Litho 4* printers, which was also in the building.

One day, while going over a job with Jack Preis, the shop foreman of Litho 4, I noticed a set of "mechanicals" (paste-ups on 172 Illustration Board) on his desk. They were extraordinarily clean and professional, much in the style of Jack Brady.

Les Scott was a fine artist; he wanted nothing to do with computers.

I asked Preis who the artist was that prepared them. "Les Scott, an artist upstairs," he replied. It was the first time I had heard Les' name.

I watched for an opportunity to speak with Les privately, then asked him if he would be willing to do some freelance work for me. He said he was available. I started giving Les work during the day, which he would take home, work on at night, and often return the job the following day.

I could hardly believe my good fortune in meeting Les—clearly a *Divinely Inspired* event. Les was trained as an artist in England. He was incredibly talented and provided me with an extremely valuable service. Les eventually left *CG&W* and started working with me, virtually full-time, as my freelance art director.

GRAPHIC DESIGN
PHOTOGRAPHY
TYPOGRAPHY
and other
Marketing-related
Services

Dean Johnson & Associates

Goal-setting was not something I verbalized; it was rather something I visualized with pencil sketches; of a layout of what an ad agency should look like (as the cover of this brochure) or of what an ideal home in Virginia Beach would look like. My sketches always closely resembled the final product.

Aerial view of the Sumitomo plant and offices in the mid-1980s. Photo by Dean. The location of the Sumitomo plant and offices suited me perfectly.

Sumitomo traces its roots to a bookshop in Kyoto, Japan, founded in 1615 by a former Buddhist priest, Masatomo Sumitomo. The diamond-shaped Igeta logo is reminiscent of a type of frame placed over a well in pre-modern Japan.

The location of the *Sumitomo* plant in Teterboro was perfect for me—just a thirty-minute drive from our office in Kinnelon and within easy driving distance of my second-largest account, *Sier-Bath Gear*; which was just ten minutes from Sumitomo. I could often call on both of them on the same day.

Notice the portion of the building in the foreground in the shape of the Sumitomo Igeta; this was offices and administration. The small, dark portion of the building was the "Igeta" room used for cafeteria, parties, and meetings. The largest portion of the building was gearbox assembly.

Bringing Bill Lechler into Sumitomo in 1984 was a stroke of genius on the part of President Noriyuki (Nick) Yamazaki. Photo by Dean.

A record-breaking achievement created by Dean, Fred, and Ted Black.

The single largest project I ever handled was reported in the trade press to be the largest ad ever placed in a trade publication—a 216-page insert in *Consulting Engineer* Magazine.

In the photo above, I'm working with Ted Black (right), the most talented writer and photographer I've ever known, and his son, Fred.

LIVES OF TWO FAMILIES CHANGED FOREVER

There is wisdom in the old adage "haste makes waste." But when we are faced with what we are absolutely sure is a golden opportunity, not a moment can be wasted.

Yet another *Divinely Inspired* event occurred in April 1984 when a clerk in the admissions office of *Guilford College* in North Carolina mistakenly sent our son Eric an *acceptance letter* to the school rather than a *rejection letter* the admissions office had decided upon.

Eric in 1984. This is the photo which we sent with Eric's application for admittance to Guilford College.

We received the acceptance letter on April 9th, 1984. We had done some research on *Guilford*. We knew that the school would be a good fit for Eric, but we were also aware of the high academic standards of the school made it a "long shot" for him.

We were all pleased when we received the acceptance letter. I decided immediately that it would be a good idea to confirm it *in person*, on the pretext of touring the campus.

On the 11th, Eric and I flew to Greensboro. We were waiting outside the admissions office when the door opened.

When I told the *admissions director* who we were, it was clear she knew *exactly* who we were and she looked horrified. She explained to me that the acceptance letter had been sent in error and that the correct rejection letter was already in the mail!

She said we were free to tour the campus on our own until it was time to go to the airport for our flight back to New Jersey. I protested and asked to meet with the Guilford tennis coach, Ray Alley, who already had a copy of Eric's tennis credentials.

Ray Alley was also appalled by the error of the admissions office and asked Eric if he would be willing to "hit a few" against some of the members of his tennis team. Eric did well against them, so the coach had a meeting with the admissions director and persuaded her to give Eric an interview. Again, to his credit, Eric did well and was accepted to Guilford on the condition that he improve some of his grades at Delbarton.

Eric competing at the U.S. Open Equitable Family Tennis Challenge event at Flushing Meadows in 1984. Photo by Dean.

By the way, Eric met his wife, Maria, at Guilford.

If I had not moved quickly, if I had waited even one more day before traveling with Eric to Guilford, Eric's marriage to Maria and the birth of their two beautiful daughters, Isabel and Camille, could never have happened! But destiny would not be denied.

A LIFE-ALTERING BATHROOM BREAK

In 1985 a man named Ron Vigneri (a sometime tennis doubles partner of mine) was in the process of converting indoor tennis courts he had built on Kinnelon Road to office condominiums. The location was close to our home in Kinnelon and not far from offices we were renting in the *CG&W* building on Rte. 23.

On May 14th of that year, another man named Ron Franks invited John and Mary Weber (tenants of ours at the time) to lunch at the *Stonehouse Inn* next to the building Ron Vigneri was converting to condos. Ron Franks proposed John and Mary join him (as tenants of *his*) in space he planned to buy in Ron Vigneri's refurbished facility. Mary, very thoughtfully and out of consideration to me, suggested I might also be interested in hearing what Ron Franks had to say, so I joined them.

When I realized what the meeting was about—that I was at risk of losing John and Mary as tenants in the *CG&W* building, in which we shared office space—and losing the proximity of their services, I was appalled.

I promptly excused myself (hinting at a bathroom break), and sprinted across the parking lot to Ron Vigneri's building in the hope that he would be there working with his father. I was breathless as I searched the building for Ron. *By the Grace of God*, I found him. I asked him to quickly show me what space he had available.

Ron showed me a suite of offices which looked perfect for us. I told him, on the spot, that I would take it. (A commitment of nearly $100,000.) I then hurried back from my "bathroom break" to the lunch meeting in time for Ron Franks to invite us next door to inspect the space he was offering to John and Mary and from which I had just returned.

After looking at the space Ron Franks was offering, I said to John and Mary, "Let's look at what else is available." The space to which I had just committed, Suite #12, looked good to them also but when Ron Franks inquired about it, Ron Vigneri said, "Sorry, that space is taken." (Thankfully, Ron Vigneri did not mention the fact that it had been taken only moments earlier, by me.)

When we returned to our office, I asked John and Mary what they thought of #12. They both said they liked it.

To their shock and surprise, I then told them that I had just given a verbal commitment to Ron Vigneri to purchase it from him. The following day, we agreed on a partnership to purchase the space together.

On October 25, 1985, *Dean Johnson & Associates*, *Type 'N Graphics*, and *Photo Design* moved their offices to 170 Kinnelon Road.

Mary and John Weber in 2010 standing in the parking lot of what was, in 1985, the Stonehouse Inn. The building in the background is the condominium in which our offices are located.

Now, more than 30 years later, the four of us still own the space, and it has been a good investment. *I credit that investment not just to a timely "bathroom break" but to Mary Weber's thoughtful, Divinely Inspired invitation.*

On July 24, 1987, Nick Yamazaki, president of *Sumitomo,* called a few of us into his office and informed us that the company had decided to relocate to Chesapeake, Virginia.

Because of the convenient proximity of Sumitomo to both our office and to Sier-Bath, this could be bad news for us, I thought.

The opening of the new plant in Chesapeake in 1988 signaled for me the start of a very different, and highly stressful lifestyle. For the next four years, I commuted by air; then, starting in 1992, by car to make the weekly 760-mile round-trip.

Helga in the receiving line at the Grand Opening of the Sumitomo Machinery plant in Chesapeake, Virginia, September 20, 1988. (l-r) Noriyuki Yamazaki SMA president, Gerald Baliles, Governor of Virginia, David Wynne, Mayor of Chesapeake, Mr. Heino, and Mr. Kaji, executives from parent company Sumitomo Heavy Industries in Tokyo. Photo by Dean.

Despite the fact that I opened an office in Virginia Beach, to give at least the appearance of proximity to *Sumitomo,* pressure mounted to pull the *Sumitomo* advertising away from me and bring it in-house.

Three people who could benefit by my departure—Garry Combs, Wade Sharp and Grace Porter—convinced their boss, Steve King, that everything I did as an agency could be done "in-house" on "desktop publishing."

By combining "desktop publishing" of printed material with the purchase of ad placement by the *Sumitomo* Purchasing Department, they argued, annual savings to *Sumitomo* could be in the range of $250,000—if they knew how to do it; which they did not.

Grace Porter tried to prove the value of "desktop publishing" to Steve King by preparing and printing a four-page folder on gearmotors on her own computer and printer. When copies were distributed, friends Jim Magee and Marcelo Zapatero both had the same reaction: "I thought she was joking," they said.

Grace Porter with my friend Jim Magee in 1989.

GREG JORDAN'S LEAP OF FAITH

"There are many talented people who haven't fulfilled their dreams because they overthought it, or they were too cautious, and were unwilling to make the leap of faith."

James Cameron, film-maker

On August 15, 1988, while our family was vacationing in Virginia Beach, I visited Greg Jordan, president of a printing company in Norfolk named *Teagle & Little*. During our meeting, I explained to Greg that I had a client, *Sumitomo Machinery*, which was relocating from New Jersey to Chesapeake. I explained to Greg that the point of the meeting was to discuss with him the printing of *Sumitomo* catalogs. I told Greg that I controlled nearly $400,000/year in catalog printing and that I was in possession of the negatives required to make the plates—that I had retrieved all the negatives from my printer in New Jersey and, at the moment, they were in the trunk of my car.

Greg responded, "I already have a salesman calling on *Sumitomo* in Chesapeake, and he should probably be entitled to any business they could obtain there." He called the salesman, who happened to be in the office, and Greg called him into the meeting.

The salesman said that he had "made sales calls on Dawn Ranges and Judy Hrushka in *Sumitomo's* temporary office in the Armada Hofler building in Chesapeake and that they had promised him an opportunity to quote on printing once the company was settled in their new location in Chesapeake."

I explained to Greg's salesman, "Bill Lechler, president of *Sumitomo*, has given me the authority to purchase printing; and I'm sure that Dawn and Judy have no purchasing authority, nor will they."

Greg then asked me if he could have a few minutes alone with his salesman. When I returned to Greg's office, Greg said, "I believe what you said and I will work directly with you on the printing of *Sumitomo* catalogs." This decision by Greg, I believe, was *Divinely Inspired*.

Greg's "leap of faith" in me resulted in several million dollars in printing business for Teagle & Little over the next thirteen years.

With Greg Jordan in Norfolk, in the backyard of Greg's father's home which I was "house sitting" in 1992.

OVERCOMING ADVERSITY

In the early evening of Monday, October 30, 1989, Bill Berkenbush (partner in *Boise Graphics*, my printing pre-press service) called from his office to tell me the shocking news that over the weekend his cleaning service had mistakenly disposed of five plastic bags of photographic chromes (8 X 10 color transparencies) and separations (films made from the chromes, including the retouching/dot etching of my customer's catalog). They had been working on this catalog for five months, and final films had already been approved by Cindy Vagel, *Design House* product manager.

This meant that all of the material for an entire fifty-two-page, four-color catalog *had been inadvertently thrown in the trash!* Time and material to reach this point in the project had been close to $100,000.

"I'm only calling you now because I've had everyone in the shop looking for your job all day. It's not here. It must have been thrown in the trash," he said.

"Let's call the garbage collector and find out what they did with the stuff," I said.

"I already did that. They dumped it in a landfill in Pennsylvania on Saturday; there's already two more days of garbage on top of it. Forget it!"

"Who's going to tell Cindy?"

"I already did," said Bill. "She'll be calling you."

I no sooner hung up on Bill than Cindy called. "Bill told me what happened," she said. "I just talked to Jeff, my boss. He said, 'Tell Dean that if we don't have our catalogs in time for the sales meeting in Princeton on December 2nd, we are going to sue him for everything he's got, including his house!'"

Work on the *Design House* catalog had begun sometime in June 1989 at Mike Tesi's photo studio. Redoing the photography would be out of the question. My only hope was that either Mike Tesi or Les Scott, had saved the "outtakes" (those versions of the photo setups that would be generally acceptable but were, in the opinion of Cindy Vagel, "marginal" for one reason or another).

Les Scott saved the day and helped us avoid what could have been a devastating lawsuit.

First thing Tuesday morning, I called Mike and explained the situation. Mike said he did have some of the outtakes. I later checked with Les and he also had some. A thorough check of all of the outtakes revealed that we had at least one 8 X 10 chrome of every photo in the catalog, albeit some "marginal" in quality.

Bill, and his partner Gerry Hartline, had begun pre-press work soon after the photography had been completed in late September. Everything they had done in the previous month would have to be re-done in about a week to give Greg Jordan and his team at *Teagle & Little* time to print, bind, and ship the job by late November.

Bill and Gerry and their team worked around the clock with Cindy looking over their shoulder 24/7. Everyone involved, including

Greg Jordan and his team at *Teagle & Little,* did an unbelievable job in getting copies of the catalog to the *Scanticon Hotel* in Princeton in time (and on budget) for the *Design House* sales meeting—and taking off my shoulders the most stressful, potentially disastrous situation I had ever encountered in my business career.

For us, the job was profitable; for Billy and Gerry, not so much.

At a lunch meeting to celebrate the successful completion of the job, Cindy Vagel informed Billy and Gerry that Jeff, owner of *Design House,* wanted to be compensated for the additional time that Cindy had had to spend checking the second round of separations—$12,000.

Cindy had given me a heads-up about it, so I watched Billy's face for a reaction. His eyeballs disappeared! All I could see were the whites of his eyes. His face was ashen, his body went limp, and he crumbled off his chair to the floor in a dead faint.

The good news for us was that by the *Grace of God,* the job was completed on time, on budget, and profitably. The catalog won design awards and we continued to do yearly business with *Design House.*

My secret to the successful conclusion of this near-disastrous events was that I never lost faith in Bill Berkenbush and his team.

Cindy Vagel, Design House project manager, and Bill Berkenbush, co-owner of Boise Graphics on November 3, 1989. Cindy posed long enough for me to take a photo during the second check of her fifty-two-page, four-color catalog after the original material was inadvertently trashed. The smiles are misleading; the pressure on this day was palpable.
(Cindy's expression says, Watch out, Dean, you could lose your house!)

Award for catalog design excellence to Dean, Cindy Vagel and Greg Jordan, president of Teagle & Little.

STRESSFUL CIRCUMSTANCES

When consciousness is "fragmented," it starts a war in the mind-body system. This war lies behind many diseases, giving rise to what modern medicine calls the "psychosomatic component." The rishis call it "the fear born of duality," and they would consider it not a component, but the chief cause of all illness.

Deepak Chopra

With Mike O'Donnell following doubles matches at Mountain Lakes Club in 1989. I had no idea then, of course, that this would be the beginning of a painful two-year episode.

I have no doubt the lower back and sciatic issues that I suffered from August 1989 and lasting until October 1991, were the result of the stressful circumstances in which I found myself at *Sumitomo*. Our basic necessities—our income and the lifestyle to which our family had become accustomed and for which I was responsible were being seriously threatened.

On a blistering-hot August 20, 1989, following two doubles tennis matches with partner Mike O'Donnell at the *Mountain Lakes Club*, then a *Heineken* at home and a nap on our reclining chair, I awoke with a pain in my buttocks which felt like I had been beaten with a baseball bat! This episode would morph into severe sciatic pain which would last for more than two years.

A week later the pain in my back was so severe, I had to default a friendly tennis match with Greg Jordan at the *Virginia Beach Racquet Club*.

Pain episodes then started to become more frequent and more intense. I tried in vain to suffer through it, probably in denial about the severity. Not until the following January 10th did I seek professional relief. I first tried chiropractic—a female chiropractor in Norfolk who, after two months of treatments, offered no relief from the constant pain.

On April 3rd, 1990, I made an appointment with a local orthopedic surgeon in Virginia Beach to whom I was referred by Bill Lechler. During a follow-up visit on May 19th, 1990, based only on an x-ray, he recommended surgery. "The sooner the better," he said. When I pushed back, he added, "If you don't have it done immediately, you will come back to me on your hands and knees begging me to do it."

Meanwhile, continuing to take weekly flights to Chesapeake, I tried various back supports and corsets, which offered no relief. I tried alternating ice and heat on the sacroiliac joint, and I joined a local spa in Kinnelon for weekly whirlpool baths and started an exercise regimen. Nothing helped. It all just seemed to make the pain worse.

This was the last photo that I took of my beloved Uncle John in May 1986.

On May 1st, 1990, on the recommendation of her doctor, I admitted my mother to *Passaic General Hospital* for blood tests to determine why her energy level was low. Thinking she'd be coming home that day, she didn't even bring toilet articles with her, so I went home to retrieve them. One test led to another, one week to another. When I was not in Chesapeake, I visited her daily in the hospital.

In the midst of it all, on June 7th, Ma's brother John, one of my favorite uncles, died. I reluctantly gave the sad news to Ma. The first half of 1990 for me seemed to be one stressful event after another.

I continued to search for relief from what was now chronic, debilitating pain. In June, I tried another chiropractor in

Helen with Bird of Paradise given to her for her birthday in 1989. "After what I've been through here, they would never get me into a hospital again unless it was it was a matter of life and death," said Ma.

Pequannock. After several treatments by him, I experienced no relief.

On July 31, 1990, three months to the day after she had gone to *Passaic General* Hospital for blood tests just to determine why her energy level was low, Ma died. I lost my strongest supporter, my best friend.

December 1990 brought a bit of a breakthrough. When I was visiting *Park Lakes Tennis Club* in Mountain Lakes one day, a tennis friend named Ken Jewel who owned a radiology lab in Caldwell, asked me where I'd been. "We miss seeing you here, Dean, what's going on?"

I told him about the chronic pain I was experiencing and about the many unsuccessful attempts at finding relief.

"Here's my card. Call my lab, tell Peggy I told you to make an appointment. I'll do an MRI and I'll call you with the result," he said.

Ron and Christa Ilgner (My good friend Ron Ilgner passed away on December 15, 2015.)

Ken did the MRI on the 10th. A few days later he called me with encouraging news: "I don't see anything going on here that should be causing you this kind of pain. I suggest you give it time; if it doesn't get any worse, be patient; if it does get worse, call me." It was good to know I wasn't dealing with a structural issue like a herniated disc. But if not that, what?

However, during the family's annual ski vacation over President's week in *Jay Peak*, Vermont in 1991 with Ron and Christa Ilgner, the pain spiraled out of control. Sleeping in a bed was too painful; only a hard floor was bearable. Walking was painful; skiing was impossible.

And all the while having to deal with Christa's constant chatter and negativity further raised my level of stress and pain.

Ron and Christa were not only friends but the company of which Ron was president was a good client, which complicated matters for me.

When we got home from Vermont, I was confined to bed for three days, applying ice packs to my sacroiliac joint every three hours.

On the advice of friend Mike O'Donnell, I then contacted a Mountain Lakes tennis player who was an orthopedic surgeon named McInerney. In March 1991, I made an appointment with him at *St. Joseph Hospital* in Paterson. Helga drove me to the hospital; she had to support me walking from the car to the hospital entrance.

McInerney put me through some range-of-motion tests during which he pounded on my s-joint with the palm of his hand; the pain brought me to my knees. His recommendation was again surgery; the sooner the better. I sensed he was seeing me not as a fellow tennis player now but as a candidate for surgery. "Thanks, but no thanks," I said.

The following day, in desperation, I made an appointment with a doctor who had an office in my building. He made an appointment for me at *Chilton Hospital* that day. There he gave me a painful Depo-Medrol epidural and assured me that the pain would be gone "by tomorrow." Not true; it offered no relief at all.

Again, I was confined to bed applying ice packs to my sacroiliac joint every three hours for three days. Interspersed with the ice packs, I tried a medication called Hydrocodone synthesized from codeine. It only served to make me ill.

Having tried pain clinics, medication, and doctors offering no solution for nearly a year-and-a-half, I began to get desperate. I started to dwell on the hardships and pain and uncertainties that my grandparents Anna and Fred must have endured to get here to this country in the nineteenth century—about the patience, persistence, and perseverance they both exhibited in not only getting here and surviving here but flourishing here—and how Anna studied her Bible daily and relied on her faith for strength. Keeping them in my thoughts gave me hope.

Adam and Elfie Pataki

I began a series of daily exercises prescribed by Leon Root in his book: *No More Aching Back*. As painful as they were, I was faithful with the exercises for several months.

At Helga's suggestion, in April 1991, I tried one more doctor—recommended by friends of ours, Adam and Elfie Pataki—Reinhard Schwartz.

Following a one-hour exam, he had no other suggestion but to refer to his brother who had a condition similar to mine; he became pain-free *only after he divorced his wife*. So much for Dr. Schwartz!

Beyond any doubt, the most painful and embarrassing experience surrounding my condition was the May, 1991 *Sumitomo* sales meeting at the *Cavalier Hotel* in Virginia Beach.

On Friday, May 3, Helga drove me to the airport in Newark. At the counter, I requested a wheelchair to get me to the gate in Newark and a wheelchair to get me to an *Enterprise* car at the airport in Norfolk.

I checked into the *Cavalier* about 3:00 PM and went immediately to my room on the tenth floor to rest. At 1:00 PM on Saturday I struggled but made it to the conference room to check on the slides for my presentation; then, exhausted from the pain, back to my room to rest.

On Sunday at 5:00 I drove to Bill Lechler's house to take a few photos of his party for sales-meeting guests, which I had agreed to do. I could do no more than walk from the car to the Lechler backyard, snap a few pictures, turn around and leave.

I ate no meals in the dining room while I was at the *Cavalier;* in my condition, leaving the room and facing people I knew would be just too painful. I ordered room service during my entire stay.

The sales meeting started on Monday at 7:45 AM in the ballroom. Several attempts to make it to the meeting were unsuccessful; any weight on my left leg was unbearable. I went back to my room to rest. I tried going out on the balcony for some fresh air but could not walk for more than a few feet from the bed. I was getting very anxious over how I was going to make it to the ballroom for my presentation on Wednesday.

On Tuesday, my only mission was to take photos of the award presentations in the ballroom at 8:00 PM. Judy Hrushka started calling me at 6:00 to see if I was going to be able to make it. I asked her to call me back in an hour. When she called at 7:00, I was still optimistic about being able to make it at 8:00, but I was delusional. At 8:00 PM, I told Judy to send someone up for my camera. She sent Gordon Carlson. A careful check of all the negatives Gordon shot, I found not one to be usable.

On Wednesday, my marketing presentation was scheduled for 11:00 AM. I started dressing and preparing for the "long" walk to the *Conference Center* at 9:00 (less than five minutes if I was healthy). Taking small shuffling steps the trip took nearly twenty minutes. I waited in the hotel kitchen until 11:00, then entered the stage via the kitchen so I wouldn't be seen. At my request, Steve King had a step-stool placed close to the podium for my left foot, which relieved the pain somewhat. As soon as my thirty-minute presentation was finished I headed back through the kitchen to my room, where I stayed until it was time to leave in the morning.

At the counter at the airport, I again requested a wheelchair to get to the gate in Norfolk and from the gate in Newark to where Helga picked me up. I climbed into the back seat of her car and lay down. Helga said I looked like "death warmed over." I had reached rock bottom. Apparently being trapped for so long in stressful circumstances had driven my life into a perpetual state of imbalance.

Dean can smile because lying on his side with knees bent provided some relief from the constant pain. His cat knew he was not well.

I spent the rest of May and all of June at home conducting business from bed or lying on the couch in a fetal position.

In June 1991, I was recommended to a physical therapist named Dan Meyers in Kinnelon. Whether he was the right guy at the right time or if my condition had just run its course, his treatments, almost immediately, began to offer some relief.

I started regular treatments and exercises with Dan on June 8th. By the 18th, I was able to start traveling again to Chesapeake—not to go to the plant but to have my friend and Sumitomo's customer service manager, Marcel Zapatero, meet me at Comfort Suites to go over assignments. The entrance to my room was adjacent to the parking lot to save me steps getting to it. On October 19th, 1991—while walking across the parking lot of Rockaway Mall on the way to a movie—Helga looked at me and said, "You're not limping." That moment signaled the end of my painful experience. After two years, the sciatic pain in my leg was suddenly gone!

At that moment, I felt my faith was justified. I had never lost faith in the belief that God would somehow get me out of this mess. That's not to say I was never afraid. But when I felt fearful, I let faith in.

THE CAUSE OF IT ALL?

The obvious answer is *stress*. During the late 1980s and early '90s, I was being assaulted from all sides; weekly travel to Chesapeake (770 miles round trip), pressures on the job to have me replaced by an in-house agency, and the death of my mother.

Stress has been linked to cardiovascular disease, ulcers, cancer, bowel disease, lower back pain, and a host of other maladies—and one of our body's responses to stress has proven to be inflammation.

In my case, I believe that inflammation of the piriformis muscle was the culprit, the cause of two years of pain.

The piriformis is a muscle in the groin that runs from the sacrum to the outer hip-bone. If it becomes inflamed, it puts pressure on the sciatic nerve that passes under it. Depending on how inflamed the piriformis is, the pressure it exerts on the sciatic nerve can be excruciating.

In my case the pain extended from my left buttock, the entire length of my left leg to my toes. That pain was what I felt with every step I took.

Here, for what it's worth, are my views of *the futility of the treatments I tried*—visits to more than fifteen specialists who claimed to have the answer to the pain—most of which I believe could have been avoided if: (1) I had known that being caught in a combination of stressful circumstances that were driving my life into a perpetual state of imbalance could cause such physical pain and (2) if I had earlier learned the benefits of proper therapeutic exercises. Only Dr. Ken Jewel and Dan Meyers set me on the right path. All other treatments were futile.

Now, with the exception of occasional minor setbacks, being relatively pain-free for nearly twenty-five years, my question to all of those—and the doctors who recommended surgery for a "slipped" or herniated disc—would be, "What happened to the herniation that all the doctors insisted was the cause and would require surgery?"

GENUINE FRIENDSHIP

Seeing the pain and pressure I was under, Bill Lechler, now president of *Sumitomo*, made an offer to me I could not refuse— to buy my business, pay for our relocation and hire me as a full-time *marketing communications manager*. I saw Bill's offer as a win-win. This turned out to be a *Divinely Inspired* offer!

After discussions with Helga, I responded to Bill in the affirmative. Bill then instructed his sales manager, Steve King, to prepare a "package" for me which would detail the verbal agreement Bill and I had made.

King stalled and dragged his feet from May 1992 until January 1993, at which time I wrote and UPS'd a strong letter to Bill detailing King's delay for which I knew Bill would have no patience.

Bill then, in his words: "I read King the riot act."

Bill knew what he was buying: my experience, my loyalty, and my work ethic. I believe he had also not forgotten the day in July 1984 when I approved his invoice to Peter Renzo for consulting when Bill was between jobs.

King finally completed and presented to me a "package," which I signed on February 4th, 1993. I then rented a house in Norfolk and started full-time employment at *Sumitomo* on March 2nd.

Thus began a new phase in our life, and the start of discussions between me and Helga about relocation to Hampton Roads.

Having lived on Ricker Road in Kinnelon for twenty-five years, we were well-established. We loved our home, which had been designed and built by Helga's uncle Siegfried Hoh. It was a unique structure as strong as a bunker on six wooded and rocky acres in the hills of western New Jersey. Our office was there. Helga's friends were there. Tennis was there.

For good reason, Helga was very reluctant to relocate. I argued that without the income from *Sumitomo*, what then? Helga's question was, "Can't you find another *Sumitomo*?" My question to Helga was, "How do I find another *Bill Lechler*?"

Throughout my career, I became friends with business associates that I liked; if they also happened to be in a position to buy my services, so much the better. Renzo at *Sier-Bath*, Lechler at *Sumitomo*, Ilgner at *Gestra*, Arning at *Supradur*, Humphrey at *Hansen*, Magee at *Sumitomo* and Bonfiglioli, Zapatero at *Sumitomo*, *Hansen* and *David Brown*—all friends. The same was true of my vendors, like Greg and Deck Jordan.

Perhaps one of the most important things I did in my career was to genuinely work on behalf of *both* customers and vendors to create win-wins that generated profits and income for both.

Deck Jordan was the founder of *Teagle & Little*, my most reliable source for printing of *Sumitomo* catalogs. Deck was also a good friend.

I rented/house-sat Deck's home in Norfolk from March 9th, 1993 until relocation from Kinnelon to Virginia Beach on November 23rd, 1994. Renting Deck's home was a win-win for both me and Deck, since Deck was spending most of his time in Florida.

The DJs on their way out on a night in 1994.

What was disastrous news for us at Sumitomo in 1987 turned into a life-long benefit *for our family in 1994.*

Bad news turned good but it took time.

OUR HOUSE IS A VERY, VERY FINE HOUSE

From the day in 1993 when I moved to Norfolk until the day I asked Helga to come south to look at a home I found for sale in Virginia Beach, I searched on my own and Helga made monthly visits and made appointments with local real estate agents, looking for a place in which to settle in Hampton Roads. For nearly two years, I was unsuccessful in finding the right house in the right location at the right price.

In September 1994, I received a call at my Sumitomo office from Janis Kuykendall, an agent with whom I had earlier contact about a home in Virginia Beach. I loved the house, but it was out of our price range, and it had since been taken off the market.

Janice called to tell me that the house was again on the market at a much-reduced price; the owner had had a buyer, but the deal fell through at the last minute. Meanwhile, the owner had already bought a home in Florida and was now in a bind with two mortgages. "We have to act quickly," Janis said. On September 25th, Helga and I met with Janis to look at the house. When we finished the tour

Helga whispered to me, "I could live here." I breathed a huge sigh of relief!

Helga and I wasted no time in making an offer to the owner. He accepted, and on November 24th, 1994 the day before Thanksgiving, we moved to Virginia Beach.

I left Deck Jordan's home, which I had been renting since March 2nd, 1993. We also brought to Virginia Beach the contents of self-storage space we had been renting in Chesapeake. Done!

How *Divinely Inspired* was this? At the very moment that the owner was desperate to sell, we were even more eager to find a home in a location, in a style, in a size, and in a price range Helga and I would find acceptable. On this day, the stars were again aligned perfectly!

Today, looking twenty-five years into the rear-view mirror, the Sumitomo relocation to Virginia could not have been more fortuitous nor more timely for us.

Our home in Kinnelon was built with the strength of a bunker on six acres atop a massive monolithic rock; we loved it; it was painful to leave it.

As much as Helga would have loved to stay in Kinnelon, living in semi-retirement in Virginia Beach has its advantages—a more moderate climate without losing the four seasons, three blocks from the oceanfront, a state park for walking and swimming in the bay, a short walk to the post office, the bank, the doctor and a pharmacy;

six supermarkets and a mall within easy drive, good hospitals close by, tennis for Helga, table tennis for me, year-round entertainment at the beach and in Norfolk, and Pungo in southern Virginia Beach for strawberry and peach farms for picking in season.

We could not have planned it better! I believe this move was *Divinely Inspired.*

Bill Lechler had a major, positive impact on the lifestyle of our family starting with a call out of the blue from Bill's boss at Hansen Transmissions, on August 30, 1983.

THE REST OF THE SUMITOMO STORY

Bill Lechler retired from Sumitomo on May 27th, 1998. This marked the beginning of the end of my employment at Sumitomo, although I managed to remain employed there for another four years.

Bill was first replaced by a wonderful Japanese fellow named Tsuneo Nagano (left, with me) who was, in turn, replaced in 1999 by a hard worker but world-class procrastinator, Steve King.

In 2001, King was replaced by a man named John Cox.

On October 30, 2001, Cox introduced me to a friend of his named Janice Greenberg who owned a marketing and communications company in Massachusetts.

It was clear to me from this moment that Ms. Greenberg's mission would be to assume control of the company's marketing and communications function, which I had been managing for seventeen years.

Ms. Greenberg started by doing a "needs assessment;" meaning: find out who does what, how much they make, and what kind of budgets they controlled. When she heard that my budget for marketing communications was over $1,000,000, the shock on her face, told me that my budget and I would become a target and that I should be prepared for her to try to assume control of both as soon as possible.

Also, from this moment on, John Cox clearly did his best to make life difficult for me, probably in the hope that I would voluntarily leave the company and open the door for Greenberg to assume control of my budget.

On May 23rd, 2002, I took John Cox to lunch at *Frank's Truck Stop* in Chesapeake to celebrate his birthday with him. Incredibly, he used the opportunity of my generosity to hurl accusations at me and make statements about my role in the company that were patently false.

During lunch, Cox began raising his voice and pointing his finger at me. He said, "What you are doing with catalog production is nothing more than lining the pockets of your friends in New Jersey by giving them work that could be done easily by our engineering department. Everyone in engineering has *Quark Xpress* on their computers. All the information needed to produce a catalog resides in their computers and any catalog can be produced with a few keystrokes." Not true. He then characterized me as an "obstructionist" in the company's system.

These were statements made by a man who knew little if anything about how the *engineering department* functioned or who totally misunderstood what he had been told by someone— probably Ms. Greenberg. His statements were so far from the truth as to be ludicrous.

When I returned from lunch I told my assistant, Mary Ann, about the conversation I had with Cox. She knew as well as I did that Cox was delusional. She said, "I'm sorry you had to go through that, Dean."

On July 29th I had a meeting with Ron Bates, *human resources manager,* at which time he offered me "voluntary early retirement." It caught me a bit by surprise but I was not totally shocked. By this time, much of what I had been doing was already being redirected to Janice Greenberg.

Unfortunately for John Cox, he could not fire me outright because of my age. I had until September 13, 2002 to let Bates know my decision, at which time I told them that I agreed to the (quite generous) terms of my separation. *After eighteen years, my last day with Sumitomo was September 27, 2002.*

Jim Magee, Sonia Bonfiglioli and Paige Cullen at Hannover Fair, 2005.

By the *Grace of God*, as it has been so many times in my life, only three days passed until October 1, 2002, when I had a call from an ex-Sumitomo salesman named Paige Cullen. Paige had accepted a position as president of a company named Bonfiglioli Riduttori. Headquartered in Italy, it had a gearbox product line similar to Sumitomo's. It was also in a market position similar to Sumitomo's in 1984—not much brand recognition, barely past the startup stage.

The first meeting with Paige was right in my "wheelhouse." It concluded with a verbal agreement for me to handle *Marketing Communications* for Bonfiglioli—trade magazine advertising design and placement, trade show booth design, publicity and press releases, printed material production and printing and coordination of their sales lead processing and fulfillment system.

I naïvely tried to hold onto *Sumitomo* printing and possibly the catalog production through my design and production supplier *Type N' Graphics*. I signed an agreement with Greg Jordan at *Teagle & Little* to represent his company, which meant I would receive a commission on whatever printing orders Sumitomo placed with them.

I knew that *Sumitomo* would need to do a significant amount of printing next year, about which I reminded their *marketing manager*. He prepared a list of some of the items they'd need for the next twelve months with a promise I would have an opportunity to quote on them.

What I didn't realize was that there was not a prayer that I or *Teagle & Little* would get a dime's worth of business from them.

Friends inside *Sumitomo* told me that the folks in control were using the promise of printing business as leverage to gain control of all of the "digital files" that *Type N' Graphics* had created over the last eighteen years. They tried twice to get the files from *Type N' Graphics* without success.

John Weber's response to them was that he was willing to give up the files if they would reimburse *Type N' Graphics* for eighteen years of storage and maintenance, which I believed was not unreasonable.

On October 8th, they also began to pressure me, also without success, since I truly believed that the files belonged to John, not me. They were now beginning to put pressure on my printer *Teagle & Little,* believing that they have files of catalogs in their system which could be downloaded to an external hard drive.

I then proposed to them a compromise whereby I would arrange for them to have one file at a time as I was given an opportunity to quote on their 2003 production and printing requirements; but apparently they were insisting on immediate control of all eighteen years of John's files.

I was naïve in the belief that they would give up even a dime's worth of business to me. Knowing now the cunning nature of those with whom I was dealing, I was sure they would not win. *I had faith in the fact that, long term, these issues would eventually be resolved in my favor.*

On November 13th, I learned through friends at Sumitomo that some of the people in charge had "concluded" that when I was hired by the company in 1993, I had a tacit agreement with Bill Lechler that he would "look the other way" and allow me to "pad" invoices from *Teagle & Little* who, in turn, would send "commissions" or "under the table" payments to me operating out of the office in New Jersey under the name of *Dean Johnson & Associates*.

Their imaginations were clearly working overtime! There is not a grain of truth in any of their assumptions. Their wheels have come completely off.

Three days after I walked out of *Sumitomo* for the last time, I began servicing Paige Cullen and Bonfiglioli; reminiscent of the offers and smooth transitions I made from *Kniep* to *Transandean*; to *Raybestos-Manhattan*, to *American Loose Leaf*, to *JA Brady*, to *Sier-Bath and to Sumitomo*. All but one of these transitions were offers initiated by others. I believe they were all *Divinely Inspired* and guided.

Acquiring the Bonfiglioli account led to contacts and business with other ex-*Sumitomo* friends—Jim Magee, Garry O'Neill, and Marcelo Zapatero. With Marcelo's support, *Hansen* again became a major account for us, thirty-four years after Bob Humphrey brought me up to Branford in 1975.

Dean Johnson & Associates was active for another eleven years—until March 2013. The business was formally closed on August 14, 2014—FORTY-ONE YEARS AFTER IT OPENED!

Peering into the rear-view mirror at my career, as far back as 1959, how ironic I find it that not only were many good friends responsible for my success but that some of the most despicable, devious characters that crossed my path did a world of good for me, however unwittingly.

A series of retirements, turn-overs, job changes and passings has left me free, now, to invest my time in "giving back."

A TIMELY OPPORTUNITY

In July 2008 I was invited by table tennis friends Tim Boggan and Dick Evans to be a member of the *U.S. Table Tennis Hall of Fame Board of Directors* to fill a vacancy created when long-time board member Mary McIlwain passed away on March 25, 2008.

Dean, Dick Evans and Tim Boggan at the 2010 Nationals in Las Vegas

For the next several years, my primary contribution on the *Board* was to create *PowerPoint* presentations of inductees into the *USTTA Hall of Fame* which are presented at the *Hall of Fame* dinner held during the U.S. Nationals in December. I was also

asked by Tim and Dick to be part of a three-member Committee which selects potential inductees. Dick was President of the USTTA Hall of Fame; Tim played the most important role in selection, preparation, and distribution of potential inductee resumes.

Being a member of committees like these expanded my exposure and network in the table tennis community—a network

Mike Babuin

which included a man named Mike Babuin.

On October 18, 2010, Mike called me to ask if I had heard that Virginia Beach had submitted a bid to host the *2011 Nationals*.

This one call set in motion yet another chain of events that would forever alter the direction of my life and smooth the transition to the next stage, as more and more of my clients retired or changed jobs.

The next morning I called a fellow named Buddy Wheeler at the *Virginia Beach Convention and Visitors Bureau*. I told him I had heard about the bid he was making and gave him a summary of my background.

Buddy invited me to his office to discuss how I could be helpful to his team in making a presentation to the *USATT Board of Directors* at the 2010 Nationals in December. During the meeting Buddy "recruited" me to be their table tennis "go-to" guy for the presentation.

For the next month-and-a-half, Buddy and I (and two other highly professional *Sports Marketing* representatives on his team; Matt Robinette and Nancy Helman) worked on the *PowerPoint*.

In December, at the *USA Table Tennis Board of Directors* meeting, Buddy made the presentation; on January 10th, the Board met and voted in favor of Virginia Beach to host the 2011 Nationals!

Soon after the announcement, Mike Cavanaugh, USATT CEO, appointed me to serve as *Chairman of the Virginia Beach Local Organizing Committee*.

The efforts by me and other members of the committee, namely Mike Babuin, were successful and, for the first time in thirty years, the U.S. Nationals would be held at a location other than Las Vegas!

For an advance look at Virginia Beach and the Convention Center where the 2011 Nationals would be held, Tim Boggan and Dick Evans, along with Tim's wife Sally and the late Dick Miles' wife Mary Detsch were hosted by Dean and Helga on the weekend of July 29-31, 2011.

The purpose of the visit was for Tim and Dick to check out not only the playing hall for the *Nationals* but the meeting rooms for the *Hall of Fame Awards Induction Banquet.*

While Tim, Dick, and I toured the *Convention Center*, Helga, Sally, and Mary went to *First Landing State Park* at Chesapeake Bay for a swim.

The Virginian-Pilot
WEDNESDAY | 12.14.11 | Our 147th year
75¢ in Hampton Roads

TABLE TENNIS TOURNEY SERVES IT UP AT BEACH

BILL TIERNAN | THE VIRGINIAN-PILOT

By Chris Carlson | *The Virginian-Pilot*

VIRGINIA BEACH

WHAT DO COMEDIAN Frank Caliendo, baseball groupie Annie Savoy and TV show terrorist Abu Fayed have in common?

Each is infatuated with table tennis, a sport normally played in a buddy's basement, but one that has morphed into the centerpiece of nightclubs in Milwaukee, Toronto and New York City.

"I was going to our wrap party, and I was on crutches because of a pingpong injury," said Adoni Maropis, an actor who tortured Jack Bauer on the TV series "24"

If you go

U.S. National Table Tennis Championships
Where: Virginia Beach Convention Center
When: 9 a.m. to 6 p.m., today to Saturday
Tickets: All-week passes, $25. Daily passes, $10, except for Saturday's semifinals and finals, which cost $20.

in 2007. "And everyone was like, 'What? Abu Fayed plays pingpong?'"

This week, pingpong, or table tennis, as the purists prefer, is the main attraction at the Virginia Beach

Actor Adoni Maropis plays an exhibition table tennis match Tuesday.

Continued from Page 1

Convention Center. With 91 tables and 562 players, including Maropis, the U.S. National Table Tennis Championships are being held in a venue far grander than a friend's garage.

The game played at the convention center isn't the game of your youth, where a wristy flick sent the ball arcing over to the other side where it was batted back until one player missed. This is competitive, challenging, and, in the biggest adjustment of all, perhaps even cool.

each of the 91 tables.

"There aren't too many that play like me," Maropis said. "I'm all over the place. I like the longer points. I call it pingpong, not table tennis. Pingpong is what people relate to. I want to bring the game to the people."

The top junior players have full-time coaches, with parents recording the action in order to break down technique. A good blade, the wooden part of the racquet, can cost more than $100, and vendors hawked equipment from table tennis shoes to robotic ball feeders.

"The big thing for most

☐ "We've gone past the nerd/geek thing. We're past the Forrest Gump thing."

Sean O'Neill, former Olympian and current coach

Wars" T-shirt. And some of the adult athletes in the less-challenging classes looked like they spent as much time eating at a table as playing

ropis, the German national team calls a kill shot an "Abu Fayed."

The sport played a prominent role in the HBO show "Entourage," and Caliendo headlined the U.S. Open earlier this year, doing impressions between points. He's a strong player, too, one who has his ranking memorized, and flew O'Neill into Arizona twice for private lessons.

Billiards and darts always have been bar attractions for late-night revelers and, more recently, some bowling centers have catered to the bar crowd. Now, table tennis is vying for a piece of the late-

---

Thanks largely to Adoni's celebrity (and to the fact that Chris Carlson, the *Virginian-Pilot's* editor, was a *24* fan) the tournament made the front page of the *Virginian-Pilot*.

During an interview with Virginia Beach TV's Bill Casey, Adoni was asked why he traveled all the way from California to compete in this event. His reply was "To show support for my friend, Dean Johnson."

Adoni was pleased with the fact that the photo in the *Pilot* shows me standing in the background. He said it symbolized to him the "looking after" that Helga and I provided for him while he was here.

MARTY REISMAN

Here, through a series of *Divinely Inspired* events, are some of my connections, and stories behind the legends of table tennis, some of whom I have had the good fortune to know over the years.

Never in my wildest dreams could I have imagined leading the blessed life I did, enjoying the lifestyle I did, and becoming friends with the fascinating people I did. Only through the miracle of *Divine Inspiration* could my life have unfolded the way it did.

Marty Reisman was one of the four world-class players about whom I read in Coleman Clark's book on table tennis in 1957.

My friendship with Reisman spanned more than fifty years. Knowing him was a glimpse into the mind of a genius, although there were times when I wasn't sure if I was dealing with a genius or a crazy person.

Later, Marty would say, "I can never recall not playing good table tennis. My racket became a delicate and a sensuous connection between the ball and my brain. The more I used it, the more dependent I became on my racket, until I was madly in love with this incredible instrument."

Hungry for competition, Marty found his way to *Lawrence's Table Tennis Parlor* on Broadway where, in just a few years, he became a world-class player, having honed his skills against the best players in America for money. Fame, talent, and his love for the game eventually lured him away from the Lower East Side, shattering his mother's dream that he would become a doctor. *Ida the Yenta*, a next-door neighbor revels with satisfaction that her prediction, "Marty will grow up to be a bum just like his father," was right on the money.

But few people have had a life as diverse, glamorous, and packed with adventure as Marty Reisman.

In the Spring of 1975, I arranged with Marty to play an exhibition at *Kinnelon, New Jersey High School*, a very successful effort to raise money for the children of a neighboring family, the Knapps, whose parents, brother, and grandmother died in a fire at their home on Christmas Day, 1974.

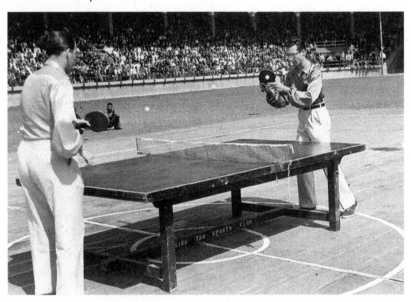

For two years, in the early 1950s, Marty toured the world as a star attraction with the Harlem Globetrotters, performing half-time exhibition table tennis matches with his partner, Doug Cartland, and appearing before a total (Marty's estimation) of more than ten million fans. Photos courtesy of Marty Reisman.

In exchange for contributing his time and talent to the exhibition in Kinnelon, I produced a promotional brochure for Marty which included the design of a logo of which he made good use for more than thirty years. Here he's displaying the logo proudly.

Dean and Marty prior to their fund-raising exhibition at Kinnelon, New Jersey High School in 1975 for the Knapp family. Photo by Frank X. Brennan, Sr.

When Reisman picks up his custom made paddle and stalks toward a table, a murmuring crowd starts to form. He hits a few casual strokes, warming up. He's thin—137 pounds on a six-foot frame, his shoulders packed with tiers of muscle, as if engineered for flight. Author unknown.

1963 pencil rendition of Marty by Dean.

For Marty Reisman—winner of seventeen national and international table tennis titles—and hundreds of big-money matches, the performance served a different need. Like many professional gamblers, he insists that neither the pay nor the play is the thing. Rather, he says, it is the risk, the intrigue, the danger that exhilarates. "Though I need it to get the adrenaline flowing, the money is nothing, the excitement, everything," he says. "I never played a game for fun in my life."

Spoken like a true gunslinger—or is that the wily hustler talking? One can never be certain about a "mythic figure," as Tim Boggan, editor of the bimonthly *Table Tennis Topics*, calls Reisman:

"No one plays with the same classical élan. No one carries the same aura. And no one for sure dresses the same as Marty Reisman. He adds dignity and class to a game that has no dignity and class."

"Yes, there is the cat burglar side, but he is a Cary Grant cat burglar, the kind of person who operates on both sides of some laws and makes it all seem right because he does it on his own terms. There is no comparable bravado figure in the game today. He is the James Bond of table tennis."

Ray Kennedy
A Little Night Music

"To come upon Reisman is like finding some perfect specimen of a lost classic age, thin as a blade, the step a matador's, the stroke a kitten's."

Murray Kempton

"Enter the prize fighter, Marty Reisman, hot from taking bets on himself in *Lawrence's Table Tennis Club* on Broadway, once a speakeasy owned by Legs Diamond and still not a joint where you threw challenges around lightly. And all at once the neon lights went on and the band started to play Gershwin."

Howard Jacobson

Marty Reisman told me that he believed he was "wired properly at birth" to play table tennis. "I'm living the purpose for which I was born," he said.

I loved Marty, but his weakness was an obsession with Marty.

The last photo I took of Marty in 2012—sitting comfortably in the "Marty" room at SpinNY reading *Table Tennis Among Jews in Poland 1924-1949* by Wieslaw Pieta.

THE LEGEND & HIS MISSION
BY SCOTT GORDON

In 1952 the great sport of classical table tennis—ping-pong—was nearly lost forever. Competitive players discovered that putting sponge on their paddles made their shots so powerful that they could win points quickly. The dramatic rallies shortened, the crack of the hard bat became muted, and ping pong was gradually fading into quiet obscurity.

But one man doggedly kept the banner of classical or hardbat table tennis alive: U.S. National champion Marty Reisman. Among world-class players, he and he alone insisted that hardbat was the real game, and for years, he successfully challenged all comers to try to beat him at the old game. His legend grew as his back-alley wins over the world's best players called into question the honesty of their skills.

Through his tireless efforts, hardbat table tennis, dormant for twenty-five years, was resurrected at the 1977 U.S. Open. Then in 1997, twenty years later, Reisman emerged from retirement and at age sixty-seven won the hardbat crown, becoming the oldest man ever to win an open national championship in a racket sport. The accomplishment sparked a hardbat revival so strong it spread not only in the U.S. but across Europe as well.

Marty's single-handed mission to bring back classical hardbat table tennis has ensured that a timeless game will continue to be played and enjoyed by children of all ages, now and into the future.

Photo of Scott by Dean taken during 2009 $100,000 Hardbat Classic in Las Vegas.

Scott Gordon
USATT Hardbat Chairman
ITTF Film Archivist

Dick and I at Dick's apartment on August 7, 2006, the day I presented Dick's Retrospective to him. Photo by Dick's wife Mary Detsch

DICK MILES

Dick Miles, powerful forehand and sterling defensive skills made him perhaps the greatest table tennis player the United States has ever produced.

From 1945 to 1962, Miles won ten men's national championships, more than anyone else before or since. He succeeded in international play as well, and for many years was considered a challenger to the dominant players of Asia and Europe. In 1959, he defeated two top Chinese players and reached the semifinals of the world championships. He was one of only three American men ever to advance that far. None have gone further.

"There was probably no other player in the history of U.S. table tennis who was better than Dick Miles," said Tim Boggan, the official historian of the United States Table Tennis Association and a friend of Miles.

1963 pencil renderings of Dick by Dean.

Richard Theodore Miles was born in Manhattan on June 12, 1925, and was raised by his mother, Ivy. By the time he was a teenager, he was playing table tennis ten hours a day or more.

After high school, he briefly attended New York University, but mostly, from then on, he just played table tennis. His signature stroke was a potent forehand using an underhand grip (that is, the racket head pointed down). Beginning with a looping backswing with the forearm held close to his body, he finished with a snap of the wrist that delivered the ball with astonishing topspin. It was his habit to drive the ball to the center of the table.

"Instead of hitting to the wings, he hit to the middle," Mr. Boggan said. "He'd go for the gut again and again."

Over the years, Miles supported himself by playing exhibitions and creating trick-shot shows (for many years, he traveled with the USO, performing for American troops abroad), and he started a company that imported table tennis equipment from Asia to supply American retailers. He was also the author of a 1968 primer, *The Game of Table Tennis*, and in the 1960s and 1970s, he was a contributor to *Sports Illustrated*.

In 1971, Miles was traveling for the magazine with the United States table tennis team for the world championships in Nagoya, Japan, when the American delegation was suddenly and surprisingly invited to China. At the time, the Nixon administration and the Chinese leadership had secretly been making diplomatic overtures, but virtually no Americans had been to the Chinese mainland in two decades. The visit of the team, "the world's most improbable— and most naïve—group of diplomats," as *Time* Magazine described them, signaled the beginning of the thaw between the two nations, a triumph of what became known as ping-pong diplomacy.

During the visit, Miles was asked to play an exhibition match with one of the players he had defeated during the 1959 world championships. With the score tied in the deciding game, his opponent, exercising the grace of a host, seemed to purposely give up a point. Unwilling to be patronized, Miles did the same. Then he suggested that the match be called a draw.

"The poor umpire didn't know what Miles was talking about," Mr. Boggan, who was present, said in an interview, laughing. "They didn't understand the concept. Finally, Miles went along with them and allowed the other guy to lose. It was absurd."

A lifelong New Yorker, Miles met Ms. Detsch in 1970 in Central Park. Companions for 40 years, they married in 1993. She is his only immediate survivor.

"We met because he had a cute dog," Ms. Detsch said in a phone interview. When he told her he was a table tennis player, she said, "I thought, 'What could that possibly mean?' I soon found out. It's its own culture. We traveled all over the world together, and he had table tennis friends everywhere," she said.

When I asked Dick Miles to what he would attribute his success in table tennis he said, "I worked very hard on my game but I really, really hated to lose."

Paradise Tennis is a game invented by Huntington Hartford, heir to the A&P fortune and owner of *Paradise Island*.

Hartford changed the name of the island from Hog Island to Paradise Island because, as he told me, he planned to upgrade the island to a tourist resort with a yacht marina, an amphitheater, a golf course, and a hotel.

Paradise Tennis is played on a table 9 feet wide, 18 feet long, and 28 inches high. The surface is aluminum painted green. The net is a foot high. Tennis racket-sized paddles

1960s Dick Miles. Photo courtesy Marty Reisman.

with short handles are used. The ball is about the size of a tennis ball.

The first time I saw "Hunt" at Reisman's after returning from my trip to Nassau (see page 87), he said, "My caretaker, Tom Donohue, told me you visited Paradise Island. How did you like it?" "My friend and I loved the tour that he and his wife gave us, but even more, we appreciated the opportunity to play your Paradise Tennis. What a thrill that was for us.

Could you tell me a little, Hunt, about the tournament you held there between tennis and table tennis players? "I couldn't attend myself," he said. "I was on my way to Europe. But my friend Wendell Niles reported to me that the tournament was very exciting. All the 'greats' were there—Ellsworth Vines, Don Budge, Pancho Gonzales, Jack Kramer, Althea Gibson, and, of course, our friend nine-time U.S. National Table Tennis Champion Dick Miles. Wendell told me that the most exciting match of the tournament was between Pancho and Dick in the semis. Gonzales hit with his usual graceful style with lots of spin and was trying hard to win. But everything he hit came back. The few times Pancho tried to hit the ball hard, it just kept coming back. It was like hitting against a wall," he said.

Miles said that when he played table tennis he looked forward to long rallies because after a while he became "at one" with the ball.

Dean and friend Rogers Case, Paradise Island, Bahamas, 1963—playing not table tennis, but Paradise Tennis, which is played on an oversized table with larger rackets and balls. Photo by Tom Donohue.

"Dick beat my friend Wendell Niles in the finals," Hunt said. "Niles had eliminated Kramer to reach the finals, while Miles beat Budge in the other semis. In the finals, Dick was too steady for Niles and he won the tournament 4 and 0. Althea Gibson won the women's, beating Nelle Longshore in the final 3 and 0."

Paradise Island 57 years after Paradise Tennis tournament was held here. Huntington Hartford's dream of it becoming a tourist resort was realized when the Island was bought by Merv Griffin in 1988 for $365 million.

The painting by artist Malcolm Russell depicts a remarkable exchange between Marty Reisman and Dick Miles during the 1949 U.S. Open Singles Championship match held at the St. Nicholas Arena in New York City. This period was the golden age of "classical" table tennis, and this illustration exemplifies the sport as played with the pre-sponge hardbat throughout the world. Perhaps the most unusual aspect of this painting is that Dick, ten-time U.S. champion, who was known for an impenetrable heavy chop defense, is shown on the attack. In contrast, Reisman, best known for his deadly attacking game, is frozen in a ballet-like defensive return.

FIFTY CENTS

APRIL 26, 1971

FIRST COLOR PHOTOS
YANKS IN PEKING

TIME

China: A Whole New Game

U.S. Ping Pong Players at Great Wall

Dick Miles kneeling in the foreground; Standing on the right is my friend Tim Boggan and friend and doubles partner George Braithwaite.

RUTH HUGHES AARONS

Ruth Hughes Aarons was born in Stamford, Connecticut to Leila (nee Hughes), an opera singer, and Alfred E. Aarons, a Broadway theatrical producer. She came from a wealthy family, and lived in New York City, where she attended and graduated from St. Agatha Episcopal High School in 1936.

Originally a tennis player, Aarons was reportedly introduced to table tennis by mere chance in the summer of 1933. During a rainstorm, which ended a tennis match early, she discovered and quickly became fascinated by table tennis.

Over time, Aarons developed and mastered her own defensive technique centered on the shakehand, a grip for which she became notable.

Ruth was on the cover of one of the very first issues of Parker Brothers' official magazine.

Aarons would spend the next five years traveling the United States and Europe, competing in various table tennis tournaments and championships, and enjoying much success, eventually building a reputation as a strong defensive player.

Her main achievements were winning two gold medals in the singles competition at the World Table Tennis Championships in 1936 and 1937, the only American competitor to do so at the time. She also won doubles and team medals for the United States in the World Table Tennis Championships. Upon winning the gold medal in Prague in 1936, the championship of woman's singles in 1937 was declared vacant due to a time limit rule in force at the time. In 2001, it was decided to declare the two players, Ruth Aarons and Gertrude Pritzi, co-champions.

While still involved in professional table tennis, Aarons, thanks to her father's theatrical connections, performed in vaudeville for several years, in both America and England, in an entertainment routine centered on the game. These performances enjoyed much success in the United States, as the United States Table Tennis Association had granted her permission, as an active member, to play the game for compensation.

1934 Champions Ruth Aarons and Jimmy McClure.

In England, however, Aarons faced sanctions by the English Table Tennis Association who had jurisdiction over her USATT-made performance contracts for shows in England, and eventual suspension by the International Table Tennis Federation (ITTF) in January 1937. Officials claimed that Aarons violated the newly enacted (December 1936) policy prohibiting active members from accepting compensation for public table tennis play. Aarons would later come back for the 1937 Women's World Singles Championships, and then retire altogether.

She also won two English Open titles.

In 1966, Aarons was inducted in the USATT Hall of Fame for her contributions to and success in the sport of table tennis.

After her retirement from table tennis in 1938, Aarons found much success as a show business manager, forming her own management firm (Aarons Management), and guiding to success the careers of clientele including Jack Cassidy, Shirley Jones, and David Cassidy.

Ruth's 1937 backhand. Photo: Zdenko Uzorinac's Table Tennis Legends.

Later in life, Aarons developed an addiction to prescription medication, particularly Seconal. According to close friend David Cassidy, he would discover thousands of pills in her home while visiting her. The medication eventually took its toll physically and psychologically, exacerbated greatly by the tragic death of longtime friend and actor Jack Cassidy in December 1976. By 1979, all her clients had lost faith in her capability as a manager and moved on.

On June 6, 1980, just five days before her sixty-second birthday, Ruth Aarons was found dead in the shower of her Beverly Hills home, presumably from falling and hitting her head.[1]

---

1   courtesy Wikipedia

For more complete details on the career of Ruth Aarons, see American Table Tennis Players of the Classic Age, Volume I. Series: A Complete History of the Classic Age of American Table Tennis. Amazon.com. ISBN-13: 978-1490573038

JIMMY MC CLURE

Jimmy McClure, born on September 28, 1916, first appeared on the 1934 American Ping-Pong Association (pro Parker Brothers) National tournament scene at the seven-city round-robin Intercity Matches at the Hotel Morrison in Chicago. Here, with a 16-1 record, he suddenly established himself as a great rival to Sol Schiff as North America's best player.

Jimmy was on the cover of the March 1934 issue of Parker Brothers' official magazine.

From 1936 to 1949, Jimmy won six medals in doubles and team events in the World Table Tennis Championships. This included four gold medals, three in the doubles with Buddy Blattner and Sol Schiff respectively and one in the team event.

When the seventeen-year old McClure arrived at the '34 APPA Nationals, he was said to have already won that season almost twenty Midwest tournaments—including the Western's at St. Louis, the Southern at Louisville, and Championships in Michigan, Indiana, and Ohio. His unexpected rise to such prominence, so startling to those who hadn't seen him play before witnessing his near-perfect record at the Intercities in Chicago—he lost only his first match, to the '33 APPA National Champion Jimmy Jacobson—clearly made him the favorite to win the '34 U.S. APPA National title.

McClure qualified and traveled to the March, 1936 Prague World Championships. Unfortunately, in the very first round of the singles, McClure drew young Richard Bergmann, already showing signs of greatness that next year would make him World Champion, and lost 3-0.

But in the Men's Doubles, five minutes before play started, the U.S. Captain, Sidney Biddell, got the ITTF Jury to permit him to switch U.S. doubles partners and team McClure with Blattner. In the quarterfinals, down 2-1 to Kelen and Bellak, they rallied to win in 5. Their semis were against the Hungarian champion Tibor Hazi and the "cocky" young man with the "quick half-volley defense and a lot of confidence" he was mentor to, Ferenc Soos. They were played on center court the last night of the tournament. Down 2-1 and 19-11 in the 4th, Bud and Jimmy seemed to have little chance, but then—with Hazi urging Soos to hit, and Soos refusing to—the steady, topspinning Americans won eight in a row!

For the U.S., the 1937 Baden World's was unique—for we won both the Men's and Women's Team events.

McClure did win his 3rd straight World Men's Doubles title—and with a new partner, Sol Schiff. They started -18, 12, 20, 17 shakily against an English team, then struggled through a five-gamer with the Hungarians Soos and Foldi. They never felt safe until the fourth against Liebster/Schediwy, and then, after losing the third at deuce to go 2-1 down to Kolar and Tereba, fought back to win a place in the final.

In the end-game, Bellak "repeatedly attempted outright winners." He "went hitting mad and attempted to kill the most impossible shots," which did not go in. Final score 21-19 for the U.S.

At the Hungary-U.S. International Match at the Stevens Hotel in Chicago, January 1935, more than 2,500 spectators set a new U.S. paid admission record for Table Tennis. Standing at the table are (l. to r.): Coleman Clark, Dougall Kittermaster, Sandor Glancz, Victor Barna, Jimmy McClure, and Ed Meltzer. Reginald Hammond is in the Umpire's Chair, and standing next to him is USTTA President Bill Stewart. Photo: TTT, February, 1935.

Jimmy in 1939. Photo inscribed to his friend Betty Henry.

In 1979 Jimmy returned dramatically to table tennis—he was honored at the first USTTA Hall of Fame Annual Awards Banquet in Las Vegas and was elected President of the Hall of Fame Board of Directors.

He now started a whole new table tennis life—becoming very involved not only in USTTA but ITTF activities. He began his multi-term tenure as USTTA vice-president and Olympic chair, and from 1984-1998 he was president of the USTTA Foundation which, in 2001, he still represented as a member of the USATT Board of Directors.

In that new millennium, with our organization's tie to the USATT Mark Matthews Lifetime Achievement Award, it was only fitting, that, among the mirrored stars atop the Stratosphere Hotel in Las Vegas, we honored one of our greatest USATT Champions—the now 85-year-old Jimmy McClure.

Jimmy died on February 12, 2005.[2]

---

2   compiled by Tim Boggan

For more complete details on the career of Jimmy McClure, see American Table Tennis Players of the Classic Age, Volume I. Series: A Complete History of the Classic Age of American Table Tennis. Amazon.com. ISBN-13: 978-1490573038

ANGIE & STELLAN BENGTSSON

Stellan Bengtsson was 1971 winner of the Worlds Men's Singles Championship over Shigeo Itoh in Nagoya, Japan. This photo was taken by Dean during a 1971 exhibition Stellan played with his friend Kjell Johansson at Madison Square Garden in New York. The photo was on the front cover of the July/August 1971 issue of *Table Tennis Topics* magazine.

This famous bronze statue of Stellan stands in front of the Falkhallen in Falkenberg, Sweden. Similarities in the figures—the body rotation, the balance, the open palm of the right hand—is notable.
Falkenberg is the birthplace of Stellan Bengtsson.
Photos by Dean Johnson

Winning 1969 USOTC Team. Angelita Rosal, Wendy Hicks,
Patty Martinez and Heather Angelinetta.

From her hometown of San Diego, Angie went to her first
USOTC's tournament in 1967 at age 11 which was held in Detroit.
In both 1968 and '69, she was on the winning USOTC team—with
Patty Martinez, Wendy Hicks, and Heather Angelinetta .

Angie won the 1968 U.S. Open Girls U-13, and in '69 and '70 she
won the U.S. Open Girls U-15—first from Pam Ramsey, then from
Judy Bochenski. In 1973 at the U.S. Open, Angie won the U-17 Girls
Doubles with Judy, and the U-17 Mixed Doubles with Eric Thom. In
1979 Angie played in her 13th consecutive U.S. Open.

In 1983, Angie went to Sweden to train . . . and in 1985, she
married 1971 World Champion Stellan Bengtsson.

In 1996, Angelita was inducted into the USATT Hall of Fame.

Dean, Angie, and Stellan during WVC 2018 in Las Vegas.

Stellan, in addition to winning the singles at the World Table Tennis Championships 1971, has won three world championships, seven European championships, sixty-five international championships. and seven English Open titles.

Angie and Stellan conduct a highly successful table tennis camp in San Diego, California called Stellangie Table Tennis. "We try to give every student the feeling that we are their personal coach," said Angie. "We're an inspiration, especially to our younger students. Many of them consider us their second mom and dad."

PATTY MARTINEZ & LEAH & TYBIE NEUBERGER

Patty Martinez. Photo by Mal Anderson.

Patty Martinez and Marty Reisman are geniuses at the ping-pong table—their brains were wired properly at birth to play ping-pong. Both have quick, "off-the-bounce," close-to-the-table games which make them unpredictable and keeps their opponents off-balance. Any ball on the forehand side of either Marty or Patty, however, is met quickly and decisively with precise "killer" forehands.

A major difference in their games, however, is that if Marty is driven back from the table he exhibits an impenetrable, graceful defense. Patty refuses to be driven back from the table; she has a good backhand block but for the most part, her offense is her defense. This instinctive strategy, at very early ages in both of their careers, brought both Marty and Patty National titles not just in the Juniors but in Adult events in both the U.S. and Canada and several-times selection to the U.S. team.

Patty is renowned for her 1965 U.S. Open finals match against nine-time Woman's champion Leah Neuberger—which she won—at age 13!

I knew Leah very well. I know first-hand what a strong player she was. We practiced together often at Lawrence's in Manhattan. She would spot me 7 points in a 21-point game and I never beat her.

Leah and I traveled to tournaments together and competed together in mixed events.

When she traveled to World Championships she would keep me posted on results by mail (as she did with this postcard in 1959).

I liked Leah and I have great respect and admiration for her achievements and contributions to the sport, especially as our historian. Leah was extremely bright, had tremendous determination and worked hard on the fundamentals of her game, but she did not blaze new ground in the sport as Marty and Patty did.

Leah and her sister Tybie's games sprouted and flourished as youngsters and, in Leah's words, "We were both very competitive. We drove each other to higher and higher levels of play and we always had the advantage of having a built-in practice partner and one with whom to discuss technique and strategy." Both Leah and Tybie won World's Mixed Doubles Championships—Tybie with Dick Miles in 1948; Leah with Erwin Klein in 1956.

Leah Thall Neuberger and her sister Thelma Thall "Tybie" Sommer.

In 1961, when Patty was just 9, her father, Jess, entered her in the 1961 *San Diego Open* at which she won the *Women's Championship*. It was at this tournament that Patty defeated Millie Littlejohn who held the Women's Singles title for a number of years. It was also at this tournament that her father realized that his daughter had the talent to be a future National Champion.

At 11, Patty won the 1964 U.S. Open junior championship and moved up to the women's division. She was little more than a curiosity when she arrived at the 1965 U.S. Open in Detroit—*where she won the U.S. Women's title.*

The genius of Patty is that she developed a unique set of table tennis skills on her own—with little formal instruction, without a coach to guide her stroke technique or strategy; she was guided by her own instincts. No one taught Patty her forehand, her backhand, the importance of footwork, or the level of composure that saw her through some of the most dire of circumstances that would cause others to fold.

"I couldn't understand why anyone thought that what I was doing was so special. It just seemed natural to me. I couldn't understand why anyone couldn't do what I was doing," said Patty.

I have observed over the years that many if not all players' games are a perfect reflection of their firmly established personalities. Both Marty and Patty are extremely intelligent. Their personalities, combined with a composure which belies an almost obsessive desire to win, makes both of them winners but also, at times, causes both to be as unpredictable and full of surprises as they are at the ping-pong table.

Patty went on to win two more U.S. Opens, three National Junior titles, three Canadian National titles and a three-time membership of the U.S. Team to World Championships. Today, in 2019, she continues to win National titles in her age group and Open titles in Hard Bat events.

2015 when Dean won Over-80 Doubles and Patty won Over-50 Doubles.

Lou performing an exhibition for fans in 1947.

A LETTER FROM DICK MILES

July 13. 2009

Dear Lois.

Your father was one of my oldest and dearest friends. As you probably know, I met him about 1941. Table tennis was our common interest and I remember going on a USO tour with him when I was 17. Prior to that, at Mitch's Club, I was exceedingly lucky that he chose me as his training partner when he began practicing for the National Championships.

Your dad was a generous man who was both a friend and mentor to me, a youngster without a father.

I also remember that in Paris in the cold, cold winter of 1947, the captain of our World Championships team was Carl Nidy, who took the players to the playing hall by subway. Thus, because your dad was a bit late, he was not permitted warm-up time but was rushed onto the table by the stodgy officials in charge. As a result, he lost a painfully close semifinal match that, had he arrived by a three-dollar taxi ride, he would certainly have won.

In Cleveland, in 1952, in the finals of the U.S. Championships, I was expected to win. But your dad beat me. I was sad for the loss but extremely pleased that Lou, and Lou only, was the man who beat me.

Last year I was asked by some writer "Who was America's greatest table tennis player?" and without a moment's hesitation, I replied "Lou Pagliaro." In recent years, your dad and I didn't see much of each other, but when we did meet for our "old-timers' get-together." it was truly wonderful to see him. Usually I invited about fifteen people, but now, since there are only three "old-timers" left—Sol Schiff, ninety-two; me, eighty-four; and Marty Reisman, seventy-nine—perhaps I'll never have it again.

Dean Johnson forwarded to me your email in which you said your dad responded with a smile when you gave him a kiss from me. Thanks for that. I'll always remember it.

Lou and Dean at Dick Miles' apartment in 2007.

Bobby in the 1960s. Photo by Mal Anderson

BOBBY GUSIKOFF

"**B**obby, let's go and watch your cousin Leon play ping-pong tonight."

From that casual suggestion, made by a father to his son on an evening in the late 1940s, comes Bobby Gusikoff's half-century recollection recounted by USATT Historian Tim Boggan, "As we climbed the stairs to those fabled Herwald Lawrence Broadway Courts, there was no way to know that in a few minutes my entire life would be changed. When the big steel door of Lawrence's opened we walked into a smoky, slightly seedy-looking room packed with people. It was standing room only, and there before me was Dick Miles playing Marty Reisman a money match. I had never before seen anything like this. That night I had found my love."

Ah, Bobby, the drama of it all, the action!

And the road not taken.

Bobby, born March 28, 1936, was brought up in a very musical family. His mother's father, Bohumil Kryl, had played the cornet for John Philip Sousa; his mother was a very accomplished pianist; his father was a noted violinist and symphony orchestra conductor. But there would be no performance concerts in Bobby's future—his footsteps would have him traveling to a different kind of playing hall.

Early in 1949 at his first Eastern Open, in Springfield, Massachusetts, young Gusikoff, not quite thirteen, was runner-up in the Boy's to a local lad, George LaPierre. Bobby remembers coming home on the subway, holding on his lap the little four-inch trophy he'd received. He still has it, though now it doesn't look as it did fifty years ago—the handle on one side's missing.

Bobby with friends Marty Reisman, Dean and Steve Berger. U.S. Nationals 2004 in Las Vegas. A montage of photos of Bobby's career is mounted on the wall in the background.

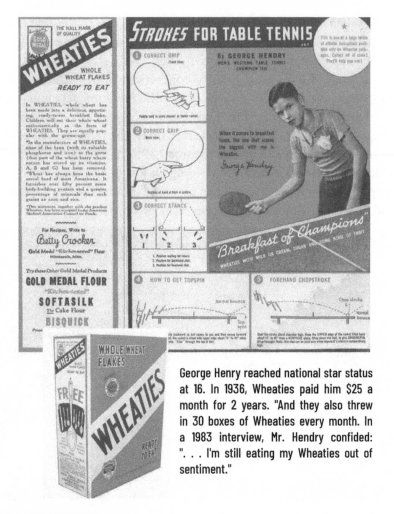

George Henry reached national star status at 16. In 1936, Wheaties paid him $25 a month for 2 years. "And they also threw in 30 boxes of Wheaties every month. In a 1983 interview, Mr. Hendry confided: ". . . I'm still eating my Wheaties out of sentiment."

GEORGE HENDRY

George Hendry won many championships before getting married, starting a family and opening a business. He then stopped playing for nearly three decades.

By 1976, he decided to try for a table tennis comeback. He called himself "the old pinger." "I just wanted to see if I still had what it takes to be good again," he said.

It wasn't easy. Table tennis had changed; a layer of sponge had been added underneath the regulation rubber-covered paddle, making the game much faster.

George and Dean at the U.S. Nationals in 2009.

"For the first couple of years, everyone was beating the hell out of me," he said. He got his game back by working on his topspin. From then on, there was no stopping him.

He won more than forty national age-group titles after taking up the paddle again.

In senior competition, no one was better—not in his native St. Louis, not in Missouri, and not in the nation.

In 1987, the Post-Dispatch described his successes with this tribute: "The 'Stan Musial' of table tennis triumphs again."

SOL SCHIFF

Sol Schiff—Mister Table Tennis—is known all over America as one of our greatest and most-beloved champions of all time. In his mid-forties, he was still in the top ranks nationally.

Sol has held titles in National Junior Singles, National Men's Singles, Men's Doubles, Mixed Doubles, Senior Singles, and Senior Doubles.

When he was just sixteen, he established himself as the nation's best player by winning the American Table Tennis Championship in 1933. The tournament was held at the Half Moon Hotel in Brooklyn, and though there was no prize money, Schiff says, "the best thing was getting to take the subway. They paid my fare, a nickel each way, and gave me fifteen cents for coffee and cake."

Sol has been on the Swaythling Cup team four times. In 1937, he won the English Open Doubles Championship with Abe Berenbaum. In 1938, he won the World's Doubles Championship with Jimmy McClure. He is regarded as the best mixed doubles player in this country, having held over a hundred titles, many of them with National Champions Leah Neuberger and Sally Green Prouty.

Five-time world Champion Richard Bergmann himself has called Schiff "the hardest hitter in the world."

He was also president of the USTTA for twelve years. He was inducted into the USTTA Hall of Fame in 1966 and was awarded a lifetime achievement award in 2000. Sol Schiff IS Mr. Table Tennis!

Sol passed away in 2012 at the age of ninety-four.

Dean and Sol at Sol's apartment in the Bronx in June 2005.

LIFE'S DINNER MENU IS SERVED . . . AT A TABLE FOR TWO
BY SALLY GREEN PROUTY

Hors d'oeurves

I was born in St. Louis, Missouri on December 23, 1922. My first major challenge in life was to survive a life-threatening surgery to correct an abdominal condition at the age of six weeks.

At age four, I started swimming, dancing and elocution classes. As a pre-teen, I swam for the Riviera Club in Indianapolis and trained as a swimmer and diver.

Entrée

In 1933, at the end of my eleventh year, I started to play table tennis. I was self-driven to excel to the best of my ability. Even in my octogenarian years, this urge has never abated.

Sally and Dean at the Prouty condo in Fort Myers, Florida, 2008.

Après le diner

Which part of a meal is the best? There are some that would say "dessert"... and I would certainly agree!

My goal, even before I was a teenager, was to become a United States Table Tennis Champion. I won the title in 1940 at age seventeen and continued to defend it for the next four years.

Although my father Fred is now gone, I still hear the same encouraging voice today that I heard, and heeded, since childhood. That voice has been there for me through all of the many crisis in my life. And what does dad's voice tell me? "Sally, it is better to be a 'has been' than a 'never was.'"

by Sally Green Prouty

With Ava Klein, Erwin Klein's daughter, following an interview with her about her father's career on July 22, 2013.

THE ERWIN KLEIN/SI WASSERMAN CONNECTION

Hall-of-Famer Erwin Klein—four-time U.S. Men's Singles Champion and (with Leah "Ping" Neuberger) 1956 *World Mixed Doubles Champion*—has been a legendry name in U.S. table tennis for decades—literally ever since that U.S. Open day in 1952 when, as an unranked, red-haired, freckle-faced, fun-loving, "chubby" kid from a California playground, he forced Dave Krizman, U.S. Boys #1, into a tenacious five-game final.

1963 pencil rendition of Erwin by Dean.

The backbone of table tennis in the Southern California area for many years was Si Wasserman. He served as President of the SCTTA from 1952 to 1955. His diligent work and enthusiastic avocation of table tennis was recognized by the national body when he was named executive vice president of the United States Table Tennis Association.

For the most part, Wasserman elected to stay in the background as far as local table tennis activities were concerned, giving advice and support to the energetic Ben Wollman, president of the local association. During many hectic controversies—sponge, anti-sponge, and so on—he could always be counted on to discuss and give judgment in a quiet, dignified manner, thereby gaining respect from both sides.

Wasserman's expert tutoring has helped develop many top players in this area—Erwin Klein, Leonard Cooperman, Sharon Acton, Charleen Hanson, and others. He has kept the Hollywood Table Tennis Center open on Highland Avenue, even on an unremunerative basis so that the players would have a place to meet and practice.

Si Wasserman, 1952.

Most players do not know of the headaches and work that enter into a successful table tennis program. They would recognize Si's worth only if his support were missing.

Si Wasserman was chief executive from 1952–1955, the longest tenure of any CTTA president.

During this period, under Si's tutelage, Erwin Klein won his first major tournament, the Southern California Men's Singles, in February, 1952. Erwin then went on to win the Canadian National Boys' and Junior Men's singles titles, the first of twenty-two national and international crowns he was destined to win.

With Si at the 2007 U.S. Nationals

Norbert competing in the 1961 Men's NTCs in Detroit where his record was 13-2. Photo by Mal Anderson.

NORBERT VAN DE WALLE

One of the oft-told stories about Norbert is his extraordinary performance at the 1962 Nationals in New York. This is an event I can report first-hand since I was a participant and spellbound observer. I first met Norbert at the '61 NTCs in Detroit.

Norbert's first tough win in '62 was beating Chuck Burns, 19 in the 5th. He then played an incredible 23-21 in the fifth semis match against Bobby Fields. For ninety minutes, it had to be heart-throbbing (one point is said to have lasted six minutes).

With Norbert at the 2004 U.S. Nationals.

Play became even more pulsating when Van de Walle suffered leg cramps and Bill Marlens came out to minister to him.

Though Bobby led 19-14 in the expedited fifth, Norby was able to pull it out, as Pauline Somael says, "on sheer guts."

Photos show that Fields, on losing, flung his bat to the table, then exchanged a sporting hug with Norby.

Listening to as many Frank Sinatra recordings whenever and wherever he could, Norby travels on USO Tours with his friend Dick Miles. They visit such faraway places as Vietnam and Alaska, where the weather outside is 55 degrees below zero and inside in the exhibition hall 80 degrees above.

At least once, Dick reports thinking their plane was going down, they've exchanged stiff-upper-lip good-byes.

A REQUEST FROM DICK MILES

What seemed to be a simple request from my friend Dick Miles turned out to be a historic day. Dick asked me to help bring together what would probably be the last historic legend get-together at his apartment on Riverside Drive in Manhattan. It was too challenging, he said, for Sol Schiff, who lived in Brooklyn, and Lou Pagliaro, who lived on Staten Island, to make their way to Dick's apartment on their own.

On Sunday, October 14th, 2007, Helga and I drove from Virginia Beach to Staten Island to pick up Paggy, then to Brooklyn to pick up Sol, where he had been relocated from the Bronx to his niece's apartment.

In an ironic twist, these players, Marty Reisman, Dick Miles, Sol Schiff, and Lou Pagliaro were *exactly* those that I read about in Coleman Clark's book in 1957—the $1.25 book (and the players) that attracted me to the sport nearly sixty years ago to the day and changed my life!

After a wonderful get-together with friends, we took Sol back to Brooklyn and Paggy home to Staten Island, then returned to Virginia Beach on Monday. A 755-mile round trip. What a trip it was!

With table tennis legends Sol Schiff, Dick Miles, Lou Pagliaro and Marty Reisman at Dick's apartment in Manhattan in 2007. 1957-2007, How the years passed by.

MARTY'S FUNERAL

On Tuesday, September 25th, 2012, Marty called to tell me, "Sometime after midnight this morning, I felt sick and in pain. I called a cab to take me to the emergency room at *Beth Israel Hospital*."

I spoke with Marty nearly every day after that until, as a result of complications following open heart surgery on October 1, a little more than ten weeks after he was admitted, he died on December 7th, 2012.

On January 13th, 2013, a burial service for Marty was scheduled at the *Mt. Richmond Cemetery* in Staten Island, New York. As much as I wanted to pay my respects to Marty, it would be an expensive, long, 700+-mile, fourteen-hour round trip. But following my theory of "just show up," I decided to go.

Many of Marty's friends were there; some I knew, some I didn't. Most notable were Marty's business associates Tony Ettinger and Cooper Fallek, and his attorney Dane Rutledge. My intention was to head home immediately after the service, but Dane suggested we go to SPiNY for lunch.

I agreed.

Lunch was courtesy of SPiNY co-owners Jonathan Bricklin and Franck Raharinosy.

This "just show up" decision resulted in another *Divinely Inspired* event six months later. That unlikely story begins on page 240.

Dean with SPiNY co-founders Franck Raharinosy and Jonathan Bricklin January 13, 2013.

On July 18, 2013, I was honored to be invited to a tribute to Marty Reisman by Sir Harold Evans at his apartment in Manhattan. (Sir Harold was editor of *The Sunday Times* and President of *Random House*. In 2001 British journalists voted Harold Evans the "all-time greatest *British newspaper editor. He was knighted in 2004.*)

With Sir Harold during the tribute to Marty at Harold's apartment in Manhattan. Harold's guests included Tony Ettinger, Cooper Fallek, Steve Berger, Nancy Franklin, et al. The basement where the party was held was the scene of many friendly matches between Harold and Marty as shown below.

Painting on the wall is a depiction of Marty stroking his ballet-like backhand chop against Dick Miles during the 1949 U.S. Open finals. See page 192 for more details. Painting by Mal Russell.

DEXTER GREY

Dexter Grey is infinitely more accomplished on piano keys than he is at a ping-pong table, but he and his twin brother Neal were worthy opponents for Dean and Marty Reisman at the 2007 U.S. Nationals.

Maestro Dexter Grey has mastered the piano like no other performer of his genre. While in China recently, he connected the East and West in an acclaimed performance.

Marty and I played Dexter and his twin brother Neal in an Over-70 doubles match on December 21, 2007 at the U.S. Nationals in Las Vegas.

Jan Ove Waldner is not a table tennis friend, not even an acquaintance; I'm just honored to be shown on the same page with him. J.O. Waldner is a Swedish table tennis player often referred to as "the Mozart of table tennis" and widely known as "the greatest table tennis player of all time." He is idolized as a legend in both Sweden and China. Photo taken by friend Christian Lillieroos following an exhibition by J.O. Waldner played at SPiNY in Manhattan on June 23, 2010.

Dean visited Chuck at his traveling museum in Bremen during the 2006 World Veterans Championships in Bremen, Germany. Photo by Jürgen Bültemeier.

CHUCK HOEY

Chuck Hoey is well known as the founding curator of the International Table Tennis Federation (ITTF) Museum in Switzerland. How this happened is much less known, and quite a story.

It all began with a chess game, one of Chuck's many passions—he won the *Sports Illustrated* Award for defeating legendary Bobby Fischer, and has fifty-seven international publications of his best games. One game he played by post some forty years ago with a friend in Sweden, who sent a move on a postcard with a Table Tennis stamp! Chuck then asked himself a very expensive question: *I wonder if there are more stamps showing Table Tennis?* Of course there were many more, and he had to have them all, the beginnings of a lifelong addiction for collecting most everything about the evolution of Table Tennis.

Chuck's collection grew to huge proportions, and he began to worry about its future. His software background helped with the next step, developing an extensive website filled with photos of the collection. Then came a coincidence. The ITTF had just purchased a large historic chateau near Lausanne in Switzerland, where they planned to relocate the ITTF headquarters. Their staff noticed his website, and after some quick negotiations, Chuck moved to Switzerland.

Entrance of new ITTF museum in Shanghai, China. Photo courtesy Chuck Hoey

The ITTF offered the entire ground floor of the chateau for the museum, ten rooms plus a free residence on the top floor, with a view of the Alps and Lake Geneva. Chuck was overwhelmed, but very happy knowing that the collection would be provided for in such a beautiful place. The museum opened in 2005. As a result of Chuck's work, he was inducted into the U.S. Table Tennis Hall of Fame in 2008.

Chuck also staged a series of portable exhibitions at the World Championships across the globe. A lot of work, but a great opportunity to show-case the museum. He continued to improve the museum with many donations over the years, and he expanded the website with more functionality. The International Swimming Hall of Fame wrote that in their opinion his website was the finest in all of sport!

A Chinese delegation then visited the museum, and soon afterwards it was moved to Shanghai, in a fabulous modern building, formally opened in 2018. Chuck was presented with an Honorary Doctorate in Education by the Shanghai University of Sports, and was appointed Honorary Curator of both the ITTF Museum and the China Table Tennis Museum.

We were all grateful to Christian Laettner for helping to make our 8th Annual Celebrity SLAMFest Party and Ping Pong for Charity Amateur Tournament the greatest ever.

CHRISTIAN LAETTNER

Christian was tireless during the two-day event in September 2016; willing to play table tennis with anyone, young and old, beginner or advanced, at any time for as long as they wanted to play. He has said, "Next to basketball, table tennis has always been my favorite sport."

Christian is to basketball what Roger Federer is to tennis, what Jan Ove Waldner is to table tennis, what Babe Ruth is to baseball—a complete and perfect package; "the greatest college basketball player of all-time." (Google: *Christian Laettner The Shot*)

Will playing at his club in Pleasantville, New York.

WILL SHORTZ

Will Shortz is a puzzle creator and, since 1993, the crossword editor of *The New York Times.*

As the world's only academically accredited "puzzlemaster," he holds a one-of-a-kind degree in enigmatology, the study of puzzles, from Indiana University. He has also been the puzzlemaster for NPR's *Weekend Edition Sunday* since the program began in 1987.

In addition to his passion for puzzles, Will has a real passion for table tennis. He started playing at a young age in his basement, as many of us did. In 2011 he turned his passion into a business when he opened the Westchester Table Tennis Center in his hometown of Pleasantville, N.Y.

Not satisfied with being a famous puzzlemaker and working hard on improving his table tennis technique, Will is on a mission to establish a record for the number of consecutive days playing the sport he loves. As I write, his streak stands at 1,601 days (and counting)!

Dr. Herbert Neubauer during warm-up in Halmstad, Sweden. Photos by Dean

DR. HERBERT NEUBAUER

Table Tennis for young Herbert Neubauer came to him when his mother challenged him to play a match on an outdoor table with her near their home in Germany. Losing that match to his mum motivated him to improve his game.

Herbert continued to improve his table tennis technique until he became a top-ten player in Germany, despite the fact that he continued to pursue his career in the Development Research Institute and later at the Ministry of Economics. He also served in the German Foreign Office as a diplomat.

Eventually, Herbert decided to leave his full-time career and to earn his living through successful financial transactions, which allowed him to spend more time on practicing at his love of table tennis and developing and producing a line of unique table tennis rubbers and blades.

Dean with Dr. Herbert Neubauer during the 2018 Liebherr World Table Tennis Championships in Halmstad, Sweden.

Dr. Neubauer, in addition to being reknowned for the development of the unique rubbers and blades bearing his name, is also known for being a highly skilled table tennis player. Highlights of his titles include:

- 7-time World Veterans Champion
- 6-time European Veterans Champion
- 4 gold medals at the World Senior Games in St George/ USA
- 2 gold medals at the European Master Games in Malmö/ Sweden
- 69 gold medals at international Championships
- 61 gold medals at Swiss Championships
- Gold medals in Singles and Team events at the World Corporate Games.

Ioanna Papadimitriou —world class fashion model.

IOANNA PAPADIMITRIOU

Ioanna Papadimitriou was crowned Miss Greece in 1994, and that signaled the beginning of a modeling career for her. A TV commercial for a Johnson & Johnson facial cream was her first job. The first few years of her career, she travelled all year to base herself in cities where clients loved to go to shoot on location—Miami and Cape Town in the winter and Athens, Milan, Munich and Hamburg in the summer.

In 2000 Ioanna moved to New York where she worked for nearly a decade through the Wilhelmina modeling agency. "It was a great experience to live and work in the same city. To see your face on a billboard on the expressway to JFK airport or on the shelves of beauty stores and on posters in windows in stores around Manhattan was just amazing," she said.

For the past five years, she has lived in Miami, where she continues modeling.

World class service to the sport—Photo by Dean.

Ioanna started playing table tennis at the age of 8 in Thessaloniki, Greece. Her mother was a top-level player herself, so it was a natural thing for Ioanna to take up the sport. Over time, her mother became her coach.

For three consecutive years, from the age of twelve on, Ioanna was Greek National Champion. She trained with the "National Selects" for seven years and had the opportunity to represent Greece in several international tournaments.

At the age of seventeen, she paused her table tennis career, but she picked up the sport again when she was living in New York. Her love of the sport has continued since. "These days, I practice a few times a week and participate in selective tournaments, but most of all, I love being part of Ping Pong for Charity, where I am given the opportunity to share my passion for table tennis and make a difference in people's lives, " she said.

TABLE TENNIS—THE SPORT FOR A LIFETIME

36-year old Katherine Wang and 5-year old daughter Katie take time off from their practice at *Bayside Recreation Center* in Virginia Beach, Virginia to pose for a photo.

99-year-young Bill Westbrook, a resident at *The Crossings at Harbour View*, a retirement community in Suffolk, Virginia, and 86-year-young Table Tennis Hall of Famer Dean Johnson squared off in 2018 to hit a few and provide some entertainment for fellow residents of the Harbor View Community.

The participation of players like Katie Wang and Bill Westbrook prove that table tennis is a healthy and fun sport for everyone— young and old, boys and girls, women and men, short and tall, rich and poor, talent or no talent.

PLAYING REISMAN

On July 3rd, 2013, I responded to an e-mail calling for someone to play the part of a "Reisman-like" character in a short *editorial* film. "Must live in Los Angeles or nearby. If interested e-mail photo by 5:00 PM Pacific time today."

Of course, I didn't live in Los Angeles and had very little idea what an "editorial film" was all about, but to me it had the potential of a once-in-a-lifetime opportunity. What was the worst that could happen? A trip to LA if it didn't work out? At the very least, I can set up an interview with Erwin Klein's daughter, Ava, for my Erwin Klein retrospective.

Our daughter Karen and her husband Jacob happened to be visiting. I asked Jacob, a skilled photographer, to come with me to my table tennis club meeting that night to take a few photos for the response to the e-mail. At left is the photo I submitted, taken by Jake Wells.

Photo by Jake Wells

To make a long story bearable, I'll skip the considerable "back and forth" and exchanges of e-mails, including one from a "stylist" when I was at the Norfolk gate to go to LA; she asked for all my sizes—shirt, trousers, hat, shoes, and jacket.

A limo picked me up at the airport and brought me to the hotel where they put me up in a 5-star room at the *Standard* where the film would be shot.

They had a wardrobe ready for me to try on when I arrived at the hotel, covered all expenses, and chauffeured me back to the airport on the 24th!

Shooting on the 23rd was long and intense. The film crew was about half a dozen—producer, cameramen, lighting, sound folks, stylists, etc.

The story line packed into the two-and-a-half minutes was about a young (twenty-something) ping-pong hustler who was making a few bucks working low-end clubs in LA. He was given a heads-up that the real money was in the high-end clubs downtown.

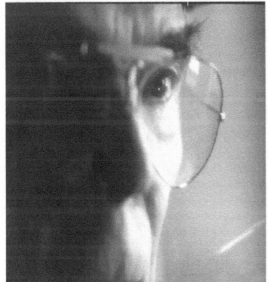

When he showed up at the *Standard* he recognized an old-timer hanging out whom he knew he would have to face.

He spent some time practicing with the younger, better players in the club and finally the time came for the showdown with the old "master."

What followed was the most difficult

The old master has his eye on the young hustler.

part of the two days for me—take after take after take of long rallies hitting the ball as hard as I could in the "match" against this young hustler.

I was eighty-one. If I had not kept myself in shape, I could not have lasted through this part of the shoot.

The faith I showed in my lifelong strategy of "just showing up" paid dividends in a once-in-a-lifetime experience and gained for me an insightful interview with the daughter of Erwin Klein, who I believe was one of the most talented players of the American Classic Age.

The young hustler finally misses a ball completely and the screen goes black, with no indication of who won the match. In the final scene, the young hustler and the old master are at the bar. I pat him on the shoulder and say, "Nice match." I pick up a wad of money on the bar, and walk out of the club. The end.[3]

---

3   The short film can be seen at: vimeo.com/75907873

The young hustler, played by Franck Raharinosy, co-owner of SPiNY, I met at SPiN on the day of Marty's funeral. I have little doubt that my selection for the part of Marty was influenced by Franck and a direct result of my "just show up" decision to attend the funeral and go to SPiNY for lunch where I "hit a few" with Franck. Of course the idea of "just show up" applies only if you have an opportunity to make a contribution or enjoy a benefit—preferably both.

SPiN LA Prior to filming with Franck Raharinosy (the young hustler) and producer Bon Duke July 21, 2013 at Downtown Standard Hotel in Los Angeles.

PING PONG FUNDRAISING

On August 7, 2009, I received a call from a table tennis friend named Hiep Tran, asking if I would come to a 4:00 PM meeting at Starbucks on Virginia Beach Boulevard. When I asked him what the meeting was about, he said, "It has something to do with ping-pong."

Kazuyuki (Kaz) Yokoyama and Wally Green playing to a packed auditorium at an elementary school in Virginia Beach in 2014. Photo by Dean.

The meeting was run by a fellow named Ken Lees to discuss the possibility of employing the game of ping-pong as a method of fundraising. The first *Ping-Pong for Poverty* charity tournament, held just six weeks later on September 19, 2009 at *Courthouse Community United Methodist Church's Family Life Center*, raised $13,000 for *people in need.*

Ping Pong for Poverty has evolved into the *Table Tennis Charity Foundation* which is committed to raising awareness of the therapeutic value that playing table tennis for mental health and brain fitness offers.

The vision of the *Foundation* is also to integrate *sports and education table tennis programs* with senior living communities, rehabilitation/medical facilities, and the Virginia Beach school system.

The *Foundation* also stresses utilizing the brain-stimulating sport of table tennis to raise money for charity partners who directly benefit those facing Alzheimer's, dementia, depression, and Parkinson's disease.

Over the years, charity events have featured table tennis exhibitions performed by some of the most skilled exhibition players in the country—Scott and Austin Preiss, Wally Green and Kazuyuki (Kaz) Yokoyama, Kim Gilbert, Ioana Papadimitriou, and basketball legend Christian Laettner.

2016 was our eighth year working with the founder of the charity, Ken Lees. This year we raised $55,000, for a total of nearly $500,000 raised for participating charities.

My role, along with Ken and Dr. Scott Sautter in this very worthwhile charity, which is now to serve as a member of the *board of directors,* started by "just showing up" at a *Starbucks* in August 2009 to attend a meeting about which I knew little other than it was "about ping-pong."

Chairman of the Board of the Table Tennis Charity Foundation Dr. Scott Sautter with board member Dean.

A FORMULA FOR A BALANCED LIFE

A March 18, 2016 e-mail read, "Date is Wednesday March 30. Six residents from *Harbor's Edge* retirement community are going to visit our campus, arriving at 11:50 AM. They will be ready to play some serious ping pong with *Eastern Virginia Medical School* students. The event is being sponsored by the *Psychiatry Interest Group* and the *Neurology Interest Group* at the *Eastern Virginia Medical School* in Norfolk.

The event is called a "Brain Fitness and ping pong presentation by Neuropsychologist Dr. Scott Sautter, and table tennis player Dean Johnson."

My role in the event was to hit a few balls and give some tips to both students and residents of *Harbor's Edge*. It was all good; all fun.

During the event, Dr. Sautter introduced me to Dr. Paul Aravich, who was apparently in attendance mainly to observe the proceedings, especially the presentation by Dr. Sautter. I later learned that Dr. Aravich is a behavioral neuroscientist and professor of *pathology and anatomy, geriatrics,* and *physical medicine and rehabilitation at EVMS.*

Dean with Table Tennis Charity Foundation founder Ken Lees and Chairman of the Board Dr. Scott Sautter.

Dr. Aravich and I made some small talk, which included a question about my age. When I told him I was eighty-four, his mouth literally dropped open. He then told me that he was conducting a seminar on *dementia care* that afternoon and asked if I would I be interested in attending. Following my theory of "just show up" I said that I would be. He said the seminar would be just down the hall and asked me to be at the entrance to the auditorium at 2:30.

Since it was now just 1:30, I helped myself to some lunch which was provided by the school. There was still another thirty minutes before I had to head to the auditorium so I went back to the student lounge to relax.

Three students arrived at the lounge about the time I did and I over-heard them talk about wanting to play some ping pong doubles, but they needed a fourth, so I volunteered. What ensued for the next thirty minutes may have been some of the most entertaining doubles I've ever played.

The students were, of course, recreational-level players. I decided, as I usually do, to keep my play at a recreational level unless, in the interest of my partner, we needed a point or two in a close game; even then I kept my returns subtle—to under-spin or soft top-spin which confused both of our opponents but which caused both of them to begin *giggling.*

After losing several games in a row, our opponents just could not understand why it was not possible for them to win even one game! In desperation, one of them unleashed one of the hardest flat forehands you can imagine—as if coming from a professional player. The ball bounced off the table and struck my bat, which happened to be angled perfectly for a block and which caused the ball to ricochet to the white line on their side of the table. The two of them began laughing so hard we could not resume play for several minutes!

The three students persuaded me to stay on the table until it was precisely time for me to head to the auditorium. As I was leaving, I said, "I've played some table tennis in my life. In fact, I was recently inducted into the *U.S. Table Tennis Hall of Fame.*" More laughter from the students. As I left the student lounge I over-heard one of them say, "I knew there was something weird about the way that guy played."

When I arrived at the entrance to the auditorium, I found nine women waiting to enter. After I filled out some disclaimer forms, one of them motioned for me to come with her. Her name was Amy, and she led my way to a table *on the stage* where eleven seats had been placed with a microphone and a bottle of water for each!

What Dr. Aravich did not tell me was that he was not just expecting me to "attend" his seminar but to sit on a panel with ten experts on the treatment of dementia and to make a presentation to 200 medical students on the subject who were just now beginning to file into the auditorium!

I only learned, officially, what my role was to be when Dr. Aravich announced from the podium that, "We have a special guest with us today. His name is Dean Johnson. He's a member of the *Table Tennis Hall of Fame* and he'll speak to us about some of the positive effects that table tennis may have on the prevention and treatment of dementia. He'll be our first speaker." By this time, I was in full panic mode.

With nowhere to hide short of saying to Dr. Aravich, "I wasn't aware that you invited me to speak, I'm sorry, I'm not prepared," I had to quickly come up with something meaningful to say to the students.

By some miracle, my thoughts raced to what Dr. Sautter had to say at the event in the morning about the benefits that table tennis has on "brain function and brain fitness."

I had to start somewhere so I said, "Table tennis is truly a game for life. I'm 86. While table tennis may be only a part of the reason for my apparent good health, I think it has been an important part. I've played competitive table tennis or tennis for nearly sixty years, and I can't think of any other aspect of my lifestyle that may have contributed to my good health at this stage of my life as much as racket sports has.

"Dr. Sautter, in his presentation this morning, spoke about the benefits of 'cross-training your brain'—with aerobic exercise, by solving mental problems, and by establishing social connections and relationships.

"Participating in the sport of table tennis has done all of that for me. And I believe that 'cross-training' your brain can benefit anyone, at any age, at any stage of one's life.

Two members of the ten-member panel on the prevention and treatment of dementia with Dr. Aravich. The program was sponsored by the Psychiatry and Neurology Interest Groups of the Eastern Virginia Medical School in Norfolk.

"*Physical exercise* is an obvious benefit to playing table tennis even at a recreational level. Table tennis has an 'addictive' quality to it. You cannot play just one game of table tennis; it's always 'let's play one more.'

"*Problem solving* is also a challenge for table tennis players. Opponents are continually throwing up challenges and questions: here's a ball with under-spin, what will you do with it? Here's a dead ball with no spin, what will you do with it? As a table tennis player, your brain must constantly work to solve a variety of strategic problems.

"The opportunities for *social interaction* and establishing relationships through table tennis are without limit. I still have friends whom I met through table tennis more than sixty years ago—including my best friend, my wife—whom I met at a table tennis tournament in 1962 and to whom I've been married for fifty-five years.

"A recent eleven-year study showed that of all the factors known to contribute to longevity, such as diet, exercise and healthy social interaction, true friendships and social interactions, in a wide variety of ways, has a crucial role in increasing not just the length but the quality of lives of older people.

"Dr. Sautter also made us aware this morning of something I never knew which is the concept of 'neuroplasticity'—the proven theory that the brain can physically change in response to repeated intense activity, such as correctly and repeatedly executing a table tennis stroke. The old adage 'practice makes perfect' is not completely true; '*perfect* practice makes perfect' is more accurate. With the knowledge that your brain can physically change with perfect practice means you are not bound by old, bad habits; it means that you can always improve, which, in turn, means there is no limit to how advanced you can become in the sport."

These thoughts led me to recall things I had heard recently about the importance of "balance" in life, which I shared with the students.

"While table tennis has filled for me, at least three of the pieces in the complex puzzle that makes for a balanced life—aerobic fitness, brain fitness and social interaction, they're not the only ingredients important in walking the tight rope called a 'balanced life.'

"Balance in one's family life is important (keep your family close,) spiritual balance is important (whether you believe in God or not, He's with you at all times. However, I believe that without God, life has no purpose, without purpose, life has no meaning). Find purpose in your work. Find what you love to do; if you can do that, you won't work a day in your life.

All of these ingredients are not easy to acquire but they're achievable—all are worth seeking because, combined, they can lead to the formula for a long and happy life."

Nine more presentations by the panel followed after which our panel received a standing ovation from the students.

Out of the crowd, I saw my doubles partner from the afternoon heading toward the stage with a paddle in his hand. He brought it for me to autograph!

I have found it fascinating in my life how a "just show up" fun event can evolve into a major, life-altering experience. On September 28th, 2016, a phone call came in from Doug Gardner, head of *marketing communications* and editor of a magazine published by the *Eastern Virginia Medical School.* He had heard about my appearance on the dementia panel. He wanted to request an interview for an article he would like to do on my table tennis career and on how table tennis may have contributed to my apparently healthy condition at my age.

I agreed, and we scheduled a meeting with Doug and his videographer, Jessie Wilde, at Bayside Recreation Center at 2:30 on October 4th. The meeting was to be divided into two segments—a video interview and a hitting session to shoot more video and still photos of me playing.

When Doug and Jessie arrived at the rec center, which had graciously supplied us with a private room for the interview and a table for hitting, I was very impressed by the amount of equipment they brought in—a video camera, two still cameras, five lights on tripods, and sound equipment. Room 1 began to look like a photo/TV studio.

Once everything was set up in the room, the interview segment took about thirty minutes; we arrived in the lobby about 3:15, where my hitting partner, Tom, was waiting.

My prior experience with photo shoots of my hitting was that they usually took no more than 15–20 minutes. Doug and Jessie started shooting exactly at 3:30. At 4:50, they were still shooting!

But for one bathroom break, it was non-stop forehands and backhands. I was stroking the ball while Tom was blocking—hitting softly enough just to keep the ball in play while Doug and Jessie were filming. Most of the rallies of forehands and backhands were twenty or thirty times over the net so Doug and Jessie could get the action shots they needed.

I estimated that I stroked the ball 2,200 times! I slept well that night.

Scenes from "Tips For Healthy Aging" video produced by Eastern Virginia Medical School in Norfolk, Virginia.[4]

---

4   The link to the video is: https://evmsedu.wistia.com/medias/beifo7h5f6

The Virginian-Pilot

September 20, 2018

September 20, 2018. Table tennis Hall of Famer Dean Johnson, 86, of Virginia Beach practices at the Great Neck Recreation Center on Tuesday. He was playing his wife Helga.
Bill Tiernan for The Virginian Pilot

"It's good fun"

*Local pingpong guru
says his sport can
keep seniors sharp*

By Lee Tolliver
The Virginian-Pilot

VIRGINIA BEACH

Dean Johnson slapped the ball back across the net with a nifty backhand slice that was on target over and over again.

His focus was intense. He moved his feet quickly to position himself for each return.

Johnson loves a game of pingpong. He says it's a great activity for the elderly, and he should know.

Johnson is 86.

"It absolutely is a fantastic sport for seniors," said Johnson, who is a U.S. Table Tennis Association Hall of Famer and has been playing for more than 50 years. "It helps with brain fitness and physical fitness.

"And it's good fun."

According to the Alzheimer's Association, it's also helpful with people suffering from early stages of the disease. Parkinson's sufferers also can benefit greatly, according to the Parkinson's Foundation.

That's why Johnson and Ken Lees give demonstrations and talks at senior living facilities throughout the area, right around the time of year

Lees hosts his Ping Pong for Charity. Events for the 10th annual fundraiser will be held today through Saturday at Chevy's night club and the Virginia Beach Field House.

The event raises funds for several health-related groups, including the Alzheimer's and Parkinson's organizations.

"Everybody has played ping-pong at some point," Lees said. "I'd like to see more people playing it and especially seniors. They always have a good time when we reintroduce them to it."

Pingpong helps improve hand-eye coordination and mental awareness. It helps get the heart rate up and burn a few calories. And one of the most important aspects for seniors

is that it's a social game.

"When we go over to (Westminister-Canterbury on the Chesapeake Bay) when they have it, everybody is having so much fun with each other," said Johnson's wife, Helga, who is 79. "There are people confined to wheelchairs that love it and play very well.

"It's how Dean and I met," she said. "I stopped playing because I play tennis. But I'm playing again and enjoying it."

Johnson has been working with Lees to create more awareness of table tennis, which he describes as a sport, whereas pingpong is a recreational activity.

"They are two different things, is how I look at it," he said. "It's the same game, just at very different levels.

"But we're never going to get

people to the level of table tennis if we don't start providing the opportunity more. There just aren't a lot of places around here to play."

Johnson said a group of about 30 players compete three times a week at the Bayside Recreation Center, but more resources are needed.

"We need a dedicated facility and a coach," he said. "Ken really wants to try and make that happen. Then we can have leagues for all levels of play and for all ages."

Including seniors.

"It's good recreation for older people and offers lots of benefits," he said. "But they can't get the benefits if there's no place for them to participate."

Lee Tolliver, 757-222-5844, lee.tolliver@pilotonline.com

Ping Pong for Charity

What Ping Pong for Charity fundraiser

When Today, Friday and Saturday. Today is the celebrity/VIP welcome party from 6-9 p.m. at Chevy's Nightclub in Virginia Beach; Friday is the celebrity SlamFEST party from 7 p.m.-11 p.m. at the Virginia Beach Field House; on Saturday, the tournament begins at 8 a.m. at the Field House.

Tickets Go to www.pingpong.gives

Celebrating the completion of ten years of serving up help for charities are: Ioanna Papadimitriou, Dean Johnson, Christian Laettner, Ken Lees, Kenny Dennard, and Adoni Maropis. Photo by Jim Setzer Images by Design.

BIRTH OF A TABLE TENNIS MUSEUM

On March 16th, 2012, Tim Boggan, Dick Evans, Mike Babuin, and I held a meeting during the *Cary Cup* tournament to discuss the possibility of identifying a location and creating a *USTTA Hall of Fame Museum*. Dick, Tim and Mike asked me to serve as *Chairman* of the Committee.

This photo of Mike Babuin and Dean with a framed print of table tennis legend Sol Schiff taken on November 28, 2014, represents the completion of the first stage of museum discussions.

After seeing this photo, Ann Campbell, owner and president of *Triangle Table Tennis*, gave the green light for us to produce ten more framed, matted and captioned photos of our twelve table tennis "Legends" and display them on a 30' wall at *Triangle Table Tennis* along with displays of Hall of Fame plaques of inductees, *Lifetime Achievement Award* recipients and display cases of artifacts and memorabilia.

Hall of Fame Museum Committee: Dean, Dick Evans and Tim Boggan with Si Wasserman. On this day in 2013, Si announced his donation of $300,000 to the Hall of Fame.

Donna Sakai, President of the U.S. Table Tennis Hall of Fame, cutting the ribbon to mark the opening of the USTTA Hall of Fame museum at Triangle Table Tennis in Morrisville, North Carolina on March 21, 2015.

Dean, *Chairman of the Museum Committee* was *Master of Ceremony.*

2018 WORLD VETERAN CHAMPIONSHIPS

On January 17th, 2014, in a call from friend David Sakai (winner of every National Senior Singles and Doubles title—Over 30, 40, 50, 60, and 65 since 1984) he reveals that he and Danny Seemiller (5-time U.S. Singles Champion) are planning to submit a bid to bring the 2018 WVC (*World Veteran Championships*) to Las Vegas.

I was pleased to hear from David but not quite sure why he was calling *me*. In hindsight, perhaps it had to do with my role as *Chairman of the 2011 U.S. Nationals Local Organizing Committee,* which brought the U.S. Nationals to Virginia Beach—the first time it was held in a city other than Las Vegas in 30 years.

What was also not clear to me at the time was the business relationship between David and Danny and the USATT in this process.

In a casual meeting with Danny at the 2014 U.S. Nationals, he shared with me the fact that he had discussions with Gordon Kaye, recently-appointed USATT CEO, and that he and David agreed with Gordon that the bid should be organized by USATT and that *Senoda* (David's company) would be a major sponsor.

So, for a time, the *Local Organizing Committee* for 2018 WVC was David, Danny and Dean.

By the end of December 2014, however, through a series of e-mails from Gordon Kaye, it became clear that Gordon and the USATT would take the lead in the bidding process.

At a meeting between the *Swathling Club Committee* (organizers of WVC) and members of the USATT *Local Organizing Committee* (Gordon, David, and Danny) during the WVC 2016 in Alicante, Spain, I learned of the good news that an agreement between the USATT, David, and Danny had been reached and signed.

This was good news and somewhat of a relief to me because, from my experience with the 2011 Nationals, I saw how challenging it would be for anything less than an organization the size of the USATT to take on such a monumental project. And when the bid specifications began to come in from Gloria Wagener at

SCI (*Swathling Club International*) I could see the tasks were considerable—even for the USATT.

But Gordon took on this historic challenge—not only willingly but with a passion. David, Danny, and I supported him in every way possible in preparing not only the *"detailed application to bid,"* but the *PowerPoint* presentation to be made to the *WVC Committee* during the *World Table Tennis Championships* in Suzhou, China.

The result you can see from this link to a video I shot during the actual announcement by Hans Westling, Chairman of the WVC Committee, when, on April 27, 2015 WVC2018 was awarded to Las Vegas.[5]

The final *Local Organizing Committee* consisted of Gordon Kaye, Danny Seemiller, Stellan Bengtsson, Mike Babuin, David Sakai, and me. Presentations in Suzhou were made by Gordon, Mike, and me.

Dean and his O80 Doubles partner and friend George Braithwaite competing in WVC2018, June 19, 2018 in Las Vegas.

WVC2018 attracted a record number of more than 4,000 participants over 40—more than any table tennis tournament ever held. Photo by Mal Anderson.

---

5   vimeo.com/126744495

World Veteran Championships Committee with USATT Local Organizing Committee: (standing) Mike Babuin, Reto Bazzi, Gordon Kaye, Dean, Michael Theis. (seated) Werner Schnyder, Diane Schöler, Eberhard Schöler, Gloria Wagener, and Hans Westling. April 27, 2015, Suzhou, China. Photo: ITTF.

ITTF Veterans Committee: (l-r) Ahmad Albahar, Zhenko Kriz, Hans Westling, Ina Jozepsone, Reto Bazzi, Paul Kyle, Diane Schöler, Galal Ezz, and Dean.

USA Table Tennis presenters in Suzhou, China—USATT CEO Gordon Kaye, Dean, and Mike Babuin posing with Hans Westling, Chairman of the WVC Committee, who announced the decision that Las Vegas will be the organizer for WVC2018.

My involvement in the WVC2018 bidding process can be traced back to Mike Babuin's call to me on October 18, 2010 alerting me to the fact that Virginia Beach had submitted a bid to host the 2011 U.S. Nationals.

I was subsequently named chairman of the *2011 Local Organizing Committee* and led the team to a highly successful event which, in turn, I believe, led to David Sakai's call to me in January 2014 to join him and Danny Seemiller in an effort to submit a bid for WVC2018—even further back than that—on a winding path to the *Divinely Inspired* event on August 20, 1956, when a coin fell in Jan Carlsson's favor on a street on the outskirts of Nice, France!

HALL OF FAME INDUCTION

Hans Westling, Chairman of the *World Veteran Championships Committee* congratulating Dean on his induction into the USTTA Hall of Fame.

SCI Press Release—Member of the *Swaythling Club International* and *ITTF Veteran Committee* member Dean Johnson was inducted into the *USTTA Hall of Fame* on December 17, 2015.

The presentation was made during the *U.S. National Championships* held in Las Vegas. Attending the occasion was Sweden's Hans Westling, Chair of the *World Veteran Championships Committee*. Notably, in 2018, Las Vegas will host the *World Veteran Championship*. Dean Johnson is a member of the Organizing Committee.

Citation Entitled: "The United States Table Tennis Hall of Fame." The citation reads, "Dean Johnson, whose outstanding service and contributions to the sport of table tennis have earned him worldwide recognition and admiration in its finest tradition."

Current Roles: Currently, Dean Johnson is Chair of the *United States Hall of Fame Museum* located at the *Triangle Table Tennis Club* in Morrisville, North Carolina.

Additionally, Dean is a founding member and presently on the Board of Directors of the *Table Tennis Charity Foundation* which, over a period of seven years, has raised a total of $323,000 for charities and people in need.

Third Time: Furthermore, it was not the only accolade that Dean Johnson secured at the *United States National Championships.* Partnering with George Brathwaite, the duo won their third Men's Doubles Over 80 title.

DECEMBER 17, 2015—DEAN'S ACCEPTANCE SPEECH

Thank you, Tim.

It's with a great deal of humility that I accept and thank our Hall of Fame Committee—for inducting me into the U.S. Table Tennis Hall of Fame.

Also, I'd like to give a special thanks to our CEO Gordon Kaye for securing this wonderful facility in which to hold our dinner here tonight. And also, by the way, for Gordon's leadership and skill in guiding us to a successful bid for WVC2018. Our membership is very fortunate to have you, Gordon, as our CEO.

Also a shout-out to Mike Babuin for his support and help in establishing our Hall of Fame Museum at Triangle Table Tennis in Morrisville, North Carolina.

Being in the right place at the right time is often not only the key to success in life but often determines the path of one's entire life.

Good fortune and Divine Guidance have played an enormous role in my life.

I was in the right place at the right time when, in 1957, I came across a little $1.25 book by Coleman Clark in a Barnes and Noble in Manhattan that would bring me to this place at this time fifty-eight years later.

This is the book. $1.25 changed my life.

In his book Clark profiled world-class American players of the day—Sol Schiff, Dick Miles, Jimmy McClure, Lou Pagliaro, Marty Reisman, Ruth Aarons, and Sally Green Prouty.

Of these future American legends of the game, many of them lived and practiced in New York. I was immediately bound and determined to find out where.

Just a recreational-level basement player, I was eager to see first hand what world-class table tennis looked like.

A search the following afternoon in the fall of 1957 led me to the corner of Broadway and 96th Street in Manhattan, a few steps below street level.

Rather than the hotbed of table tennis I had expected, the place was dark except for a bare bulb above a desk to the left of the entrance at which sat a 30-something-year-old man to whom I said, "Hi; my name is Dean. Is this the place where the good players play?" He never answered my question. Instead he just said, "You want to play?" I said, "No thanks, I just want to see good players play."

"I Bernie Bukiet," he said. "I your national champion" You have big country here. How come you can't find someone to beat me?" (I learned later that Bernie had just won the Men's Singles in South Bend.)

I ended up staying until nearly dawn the next day watching Miles, Reisman, Bukiet, Cartland, Bobby Gusikoff, Leah Neuberger, and Pauline Somael battle in the most amazing display of table tennis I had ever seen. I was hooked!

Because table tennis, with just 2,500 registered players at the time, it was really a subculture compared to sports like baseball, football, and basketball. I was so excited by what I had seen, I remember wondering at the time, "If I worked really hard, could I be somebody in this game?"

This night turned out to be life-altering for me. It began an incredible adventure which brought me together with Helga, whom I met at the Canadian Nationals in 1962, brought three beautiful children into the world, and introduced me to the great sport of table tennis, to a wonderful group of people, many of whom have become close friends.

Incredibly, in addition, nearly every business client I had after the late 1960s was directly or indirectly connected to table tennis— and that continued for more than forty years.

One of my proudest achievements is the six-volume history set covering 1931–1966 that I compiled over ten years. This was a period in which an American woman won two world's singles championships, three American men won three world's doubles championships, two American women and two American men won two Worlds Mixed Doubles Championships, three American men advanced to the semi-finals in World Championships and one American teenager was the youngest ever to win a U.S. Open Championship. This period in our history should not be forgotten.

I use the word "compiled" here in putting this set together because most of the credit for this series goes to my friend Tim Boggan—for the records he kept, for the writing he did, and to Mal Anderson and his photographs, which preserve the history of our sport. They have both contributed mightily to this unique period in American table tennis history and they continue to contribute. My contribution was only to do the things I love in bringing it all together in published form—which is what I did in my career.

My plan now, in "semi"-retirement, is to continue to promote events for veteran players nationwide and to continue to promote the health benefits of our sport—especially to senior citizens— physical fitness and brain fitness along with a healthy lifestyle. It has been clinically proven that regular participation in table tennis promotes a more balanced and happier life.

As you have seen, table tennis has had a profound impact on my life for nearly sixty years. I have our great sport to thank for all I have, and I have you to thank, my friends here, for making this such a wonderful evening for me. And I share it, as I have my life for fifty-three years, with my dear wife Helga.

It is a joy and a privilege for me to again be at the right place at the right time in my life to receive this honor tonight.

You have all made me very proud. I'm honored beyond words to receive this award. I'm deeply honored to be in the company of other Hall of Fame contributors and officials and to be even mentioned in the same breath with Hall of Fame Players.

Thank you.

As I stepped off the stage I wondered to myself "Have I become somebody in this sport I love?" I don't know the answer to that, but I believe I've made more of an impression than I ever imagined I would.

In addition to a career spanning nearly sixty years in the sport, the accomplishments for which Dean was inducted include:

In 2011 he was *Chairman of the Local Organizing Committee* which brought the *U.S. National Table Tennis Championships* to Virginia Beach and for which he was named *Ambassador Extraordinaire* by the City.

He is also a member of the *ITTF Veterans Committee*, a member of a Committee which established an *All-America Over-40 Tour*, a member of the Committee which recently won a bid to bring the *World Veteran Championships* to Las Vegas in 2018 and Chairman of a committee which established a USTTA Hall of Fame Museum in Morrisville, North Carolina.

Johnson was recently named a member of the prestigious *Swaythling Club International*, he's a founding member and on the Board of Directors of the *Table Tennis Charity Foundation* which, in 2018, has raised nearly $600,000 for organizations and people in need and he is publisher of a six-volume set: *World Class American Table Tennis Players of the Classic Age—1931–1966* and a memoir: *How The Years Passed By.*

With doubles partner and friend
George Braithwaite.

Bonus 14-minute film highlighting World Class American Table Tennis

Dick Miles 10-time U.S. Men's Singles Champion
Leah Neuberger 9-time U.S. Women's Singles Champion
Lou Pagliaro 4-time U.S. Men's Singles Champion
Marty Reisman 2-time U.S. Men's Singles Champ
Bobby Gusikoff 1959 Men's Singles Champion
Mr. Herwald Lawrence narrator of the film and famous proprietor of 2 New York table tennis courts

BACKSTORY

In December 2018, I stumbled upon a film that had been stored in a carton in a crawl space in our house for more than 25 years and before that in our garage in New Jersey. It's a short film clip ironically titled: "Table For Two."

The film was shot at the famous Broadway Table Tennis Courts at 54th Street in Manhattan. It was on the level, not of a professional film but a very good home movie. It is narrated by the legendary proprietor of the Courts named Herwald Lawrence. Mr. Lawrence, shown in the lower left panel of the graphic, was later proprietor of the courts at 96th street and Broadway. (Mr. Lawrence, by the way, is the man from whom I received weekly table tennis lessons at the 96th Street Courts in 1957.) The "plot" of the film is about a wife who is unhappy with staying home every night and is looking for something different to do for the evening. The husband decides on going to a table tennis parlor to watch matches. When he calls for reservations he says in a voice loud enough for his wife to hear: "I would like to make a reservation for a table for two." Of course the wife is very disappointed when she learns they're not going to a nice New York restaurant for dinner.

Based on the players who appear in the film, (all of whom I knew, all of whom have become legends of the sport and who are featured in this book, and many with whom I had become close friends over the years) the film was produced in 1954.

The film is 14 minutes long. Much of the 14 minutes is exciting, action-packed competition and exhibition table tennis by five of the WORLD'S greatest players of the Classic Age, both male and female.

Here's the link to Table For Two.

Just copy and paste it to your browser and enjoy the film. https://vimeo.com/315003766/e1614e7fb9

Dean Johnson

LIFE'S LESSONS LEARNED

• Do the things you love and you'll never work a day in your life. *Actress Betty White, who turned ninety-six four days before I turned eighty-six, agrees. She says she loves to work. "I'll stop working when they stop asking," she says. (She calls what she does "work" but she loves what she does.)*

• Confidence morphing into overconfidence; humility morphing into arrogance is a formula for failure.

• Develop good daily habits, they'll work for you every day.

• Longevity is connected to balance—balance in one's family life, one's social life, one's working life, one's spiritual life, financial life, diet, and physical fitness. It's a delicate balance that requires discipline. Having all of them in your life offers no guarantee of longevity but maintaining balance greatly improves one's chances for a long and happy life.

• A recent study showed that of all the factors known to contribute to longevity such as diet, exercise, and healthy social interaction, true friendships and social interactions ranked the highest.

• To achieve something: this evening, plan your work; tomorrow morning. start working your plan.

• Without God, life has no purpose. Without purpose, life has no meaning.

• Nearly every man to whom I reported in my career is gone. I loved each of them but they all suffered, I believe, either from a disproportionate focus on symbolism or, in retirement, the devastating effects of a loss of mission and purpose in their lives.

• Coincidence is God's way of remaining anonymous.

You are who you are for a reason.
You're part of an intricate plan.
You're a precious and perfect unique design,
Called God's special woman or man.
You look like you look for a reason.
Our God made no mistake.
He knit you together within the womb.
You're just what He wanted to make.
The parents you had were the ones He chose,
And no matter how you may feel,
Thety were custom-designed with God's plan in mind,
And they bear the Master's seal.
No, that trauma you faced was not easy.
And God wept that it hurt you so;
But it was allowed to shape your heart
So that into His likeness you'd grow.
You are who you are for a reason,
You've been formed by the Master's rod.
You are who you are, beloved,
Because there is a God!
by *Russell Kelfer*

WHO'S WHO

Johnson/Bültemeier

Friends

World Class Achievers

When God-given talent and a recognition of the gift they were given are combined with hard work, dedication, and perseverance; when a talent is combined with a love and a passion for what they believe; if the talent is combined with the good fortune of being introduced to a mentor early in life who is willing to take a young bird under his or her wing; when talent is combined with the good fortune of being

WHO'S WHO

Donohue, Coates/Brennan

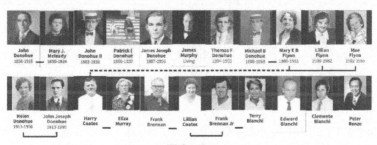

Friends

World Class Achievers

born to parents who are supportive and have the time and resources to invest in them; when talent is motivated and driven by a hunger for success, the talent may then live the meaning behind the lyrics of the Louis Armstrong song: "It comes out if it's in you, yes indeed."

Dean Johnson

ACKNOWLEDGMENTS

I was guided on my path by my mother Helen Donohue Johnson and my grandmother Anna M. Johnson, who, by their example, were a spiritual beacon and inspiration; by my uncle John Donohue, who loved me and showed it when he gave me a stern lecture when he heard from my mother that I planned to quit school at sixteen; by Vic Johnson and Phyllis Brady, who, not by their words but by their deeds, helped pave the way for me to make use of the limited talents that I was given; by Jack Brady, who, despite his treacherous and ruthless nature, led the way to my first employment at Kniep's ad agency; by Louis Kniep, who brought me not only into his business but treated me like a son; by Heinrich and Erika Bültemeier who so lovingly and graciously accepted me into their family; by Peter Renzo, who not only brought me into Sier-Bath but accepted me as a member of the Sier-Bath family; and last but not least, by Bill Lechler, who not only brought me into Sumitomo as an ad agent but had my back during the turbulent '90s and paved the way for me to be a Sumitomo employee by acquiring our business and facilitating our relocation to Virginia Beach.

Today, many of those who helped bring me to where I am are gone, but I continue to be guided by my Heavenly Father—by the Divine Intelligence that I believe permeates the universe, which is as real to me as the earthly guides. All of them appeared in my life at precisely the right time and led me to this time and place in my life.
                                                                    —Dean Johnson

"You put the words together, and you hope they're in the right order. If they are, perhaps you gave the world a nudge."
                                                                    —Unknown

Special thanks to my mother, Helen Donohue Johnson, who preserved the articles, photographs, and journals which help tell the story of my life and, by her example, encouraged me to do the same.

To my wife, my inspiration: Helga Johnson.
Thanks also to many of my relatives and friends who paved the way for me through their generosity, wisdom and by their example.

To my Grand Uncle Jimmy Donohue, Eliza Murray, Lillian (Coates) Brennan, Frank Brennan Sr., Frank Brennan, Jr., Philip Graham Vance, Jan Carlsson, Herwald Lawrence, Sol Schiff, Marty Reisman, Dick Miles, Mel Schnall, Clementi J. Bianchi, Joe Murphy, Bob Humphrey, John and Mary Weber, Les Scott, Noriyuki (Nick) Yamazaki, Marcelo Zapatero, Ted Black, Greg Jordan, Deck Jordan, Ron Ilgner, Holger Arning, Bill Berken-bush, Jim Magee,Tim Boggan, Dick Evans, Harold Evans, Mike Babuin, Jacob Wells, Hiep Tran, Ken Lees, Scott Sautter, David Sakai, Dan Seemiller, and Gordon Kaye.

Grateful for images on the following pages:
Page 6: Bing.com/images
Pages 8: Religious and philosophical views of Albert Einstein. Wikipedia
Pages 93: Mal Anderson
Page 269: Poem by Russell Kelfer
All other images courtesy of the author